WEDE...
...ur

BY (

SUSAN

S.COM
US.COM

With grateful thanks to Carl R. Mueller, whose
fascinating introductions to his translations of the
Greek and German playwrights provided
inspiration for this series.

Published by In an Hour Books
an imprint of Smith and Kraus, Inc.
177 Lyme Road, Hanover, NH 03755
inanhourbooks.com SmithandKraus.com

Know the playwright, love the play.

In an Hour, In a Minute, and Theater IQ are registered trademarks of
In an Hour Books.

Front cover design by Dan Mehling, dmehling@gmail.com
Text design by Kate Mueller, Electric Dragon Productions
Book production by Dede Cummings Design, DCDesign@sover.net

ISBN-13: 978-1-936232-29-1
ISBN-10: 1-936232-29-4
Library of Congress Control Number: 200994321

CONTENTS

Why Playwrights in an Hour?

This new series by Smith and Kraus Publishers titled Playwrights in an Hour has a dual purpose for being: one academic, the other general. For the general reader, this volume, as well as the many others in the series, offers in compact form the information needed for a basic understanding and appreciation of the works of each volume's featured playwright. Which is not to say that there don't exist volumes on end devoted to each playwright under consideration. But inasmuch as few are blessed with enough time to read the splendid scholarship that is available, a brief, highly focused accounting of the playwright's life and work is in order. The central feature of the series, a thirty- to forty-page essay, integrates the playwright into the context of his or her time and place. The volumes, though written to high standards of academic integrity, are accessible in style and approach to the general reader as well as to the student and, of course, to the theater professional and theatergoer. These books will serve for the brushing up of one's knowledge of a playwright's career, to the benefit of theater work or theatergoing. The Playwrights in an Hour series represents all periods of Western theater: Aeschylus to Shakespeare to Wedekind to Ibsen to Williams to Beckett, and on to the great contemporary playwrights who continue to offer joy and enlightenment to a grateful world.

Carl R. Mueller
School of Theater, Film and Television
Department of Theater
University of California, Los Angeles

Introduction

I t is an irony of literature that one of the wildest and most erotic of German dramatists should have been named after one of America's most mild-mannered moralists, the Philadelphian diplomat whom D. H. Lawrence liked to disdain as "snuff-colored Ben Franklin."

Benjamin Franklin Wedekind was anything but "snuff-colored." He shared with D. H. Lawrence a compulsion to probe the dark corners of the human libido, the secret currents flowing under the rational surface of bourgeois life. Sigmund Freud, Richard von Kraft-Ebing, and others were also writing about sex during this straitlaced time, in a Germany that was arguably the most repressed state in Europe. Although Wedekind shared with these men a conviction that suppressing one's sexual urges could lead to tragic consequences, Wedekind's purposes were hardly theoretical or therapeutic. He was to sexual provocation what Mikhail Bakunin, the Russian anarchist, was to political provocation: an extremist on behalf of absolute freedom, which sometimes made him, like Bakunin, look like a social outlaw.

Wedekind's two Lulu plays (*Earth Spirit* and *Pandora's Box*) are the best examples of his moral anarchy, which is why they still have the power to alienate audiences. (Lee Breuer's 1981 production of this duo in the second season of the American Repertory Theatre lost us half our subscribers!). Lulu is a totally amoral courtesan, who follows her desires regardless of moral, spiritual, or canonical laws. In her mind, sex is a form of power as well as pleasure, which is why Wedekind's poetic justice, at the end of *Pandora's Box,* is to have Lulu in London murdered by Jack the Ripper, who thereupon cuts out her vulva, washes his hands in a bucket, and leaves the stage, muttering "I'm so lucky. I'm so lucky."

Wedekind's other erotic masterpiece is *Spring Awakening,* a play about the tragic flowering of adolescent sexual desire in a time without sexual enlightenment. A number of young people in this play suffer either death or imprisonment because their parents and teachers have not yet learned how to cope with natural human instincts. Though this topic may seem passé, the recent success of *Spring Awakening* as a Broadway musical suggests that adolescent sexuality is still very much an important social issue.

Stylistically, the greatest influence on Wedekind was Georg Buechner, that strange post-modern prodigy of the early nineteenth-century Romantic stage, who wrote about the underside of human character when his German contemporaries were preoccupied with outlandish heroic actions and flamboyant royal personages. If Buechner was Wedekind's immediate predecessor, his greatest follower was probably the early Bertolt Brecht of *Baal, In the Jungle of Cities,* and *Drums in the Night,* when Brecht's plays were still being lit by flashes of existential lightning rather than by political signal fires.

And of course, Wedekind's influence could later be found in such films as *Zero de Conduite, The Last Laugh,* and particularly *The Blue Angel,* which seems like a cinematic version of *Earth Spirit* with Marlene Dietrich in the part of Lulu.

Though his name is less familiar than his namesake, Benjamin Franklin Wedekind still had the courage to write his own Declaration of Independence. As W. B. Yeats said of Jonathan Swift, he served human liberty.

Robert Brustein
Founding Director of the Yale and American Repertory Theatres
Distinguishing Scholar in Residence, Suffolk University

Wedekind

IN A MINUTE

AGE	DATE	
—	1864	**Enter Benjamin Franklin Wedekind.**
2	1866	Fyodor Dostoevsky — *Crime and Punishment*
4	1868	The game of badminton is invented in Gloucestershire, England.
5	1869	Debtors prisons are abolished in England.
7	1871	Stanley meets Livingstone at Ujiji.
8	1872	Jules Verne — *Around the World in Eighty Days*
10	1874	Winston Churchill is born.
11	1875	Mark Twain — *The Adventures of Tom Sawyer*
12	1876	Johannes Brahms — Symphony No. 1
14	1878	Gilbert and Sullivan — *H.M.S. Pinafore*
18	1882	Berlin Philharmonic Orchestra is founded.
21	1885	Germany annexes Tanganyika and Zanzibar.
22	1886	Grover Cleveland unveils the Statue of Liberty, a gift from France.
23	1887	August Strindberg — *The Father*
26	1890	Oscar Wilde — *The Picture of Dorian Gray*
28	1892	Pyotr Ilyich Tchaikovsky — *The Nutcracker*
32	1896	Anton Chekhov — *The Seagull*
33	1897	Theodore Herzl holds first Zionist Congress in Basel, Switzerland.
34	**1898**	**Frank Wedekind — *Earth Spirit***
35	1899	Henrik Ibsen — *When We Dead Awaken*
36	**1900**	**Frank Wedekind — *The Love Potion***
37	**1901**	**Frank Wedekind — *The Marquis of Keith***
38	1902	Leon Trotsky escapes from a Siberian prison, settles in London.
40	**1904**	**Frank Wedekind — *Pandora's Box, a Monster Tragedy***
42	**1906**	**Frank Wedekind — *Spring Awakening***
44	**1908**	**Frank Wedekind — *Censorship***
48	1912	Arthur Schnitzler — *Professor Bernhardi*
49	**1913**	**Frank Wedekind — *Samson***
51	1915	Germany blockades England as part of its World War I strategy.
53	**1918**	**Exit Frank Wedekind.**

A snapshot of the playwright's world. From historical events to pop-culture and the literary landscape of the time, this brief list catalogues events that directly or indirectly impacted the playwright's writing. Play citations refer to premiere dates.

Wedekind

DRAMATIC WORKS

Little Hans (Der Kleine Hans)

The Quick-Sketch Artist, or Art and Mammon (Der Schnellmaler, oder Kunst und Mammon)

Elin's Awakening (Elins Erweckung)

Children and Fools, or The World of Youth (Kinder und Narren, oder Die junge Welt)

Spring's Awakening: A Children's Tragedy (Frühlings Erwachen: Eine Kindertragödie)

The Love Potion (Der Liebestrank)

Pandora's Box: A Monster Tragedy (Die Büchse der Pandora: Eine Monstretragödie)

The Solar Spectrum (Das Sonnenspektrum)

Earth Spirit (Erdgeist)

The Tenor (Die Kammersänger)

The Marquis of Keith (Der Marquis von Keith)

Pandora's Box (Die Büchse der Pandora)

Such Is Life, or King Nicolo (So Ist Das Leben, oder König Nicolo)

The Empress of Newfoundland (Die Kaiserin von Neufundland)

Hidalla, or Karl Hetmann, the Dwarf-Giant (Hidalla, oder Karl Hetman Der Zwergriese)

Death and Devil, previously titled *The Dance of Death (Totentanz, oder Tod und Teufel)*

Music (Musik)

Censorship (Die Zensur)

Oaha, the Satire on Satire, or Till, the Owlglass (Oaha, die Satire der Satire, oder Till Eulenspiegel)

This section presents a complete list of the playwright's works in chronological order. Titles appearing in another language indicate that they were first written and premiered in that language.

The Philosopher's Stone (Der Stein der Weisen)
Castle Wetterstein (Schloss Wetterstein)
Francesca (Franziska)
Samson, or Shame and Jealousy (Simson, oder Scham und Eifersucht)
Bismarck
Superfearless (Überfürchtenichts)
Hercules (Herakles)
Felix and Galathea (Felix und Galathea)

NARRATIVE PROSE

Mine-Haha: On the Bodily Education of Young Girls (Mine-Haha oder
           über die körperliche Erziehung der jungen Mädchen)
Princess Russalka (Die Fürstin Russalka)
Rabbi Esra
An Evil Demon
Flirting
The Seducer
I'm Bored
The First Step
Love at First Glance (Die Liebe auf den ersten Blick)
The Sacrificial Lamb (Das Opferlamm)
Marianne
Bella
Diary of an Erotic Life (Die Tagebücher: ein erotisches Leben) (1887–1918)

CRITICAL PROSE

The Art of Acting: A Glossary (Schauspielkunst: Eine Glossarium)
Thoughts on the Circus
A Dangerous Individual
Ibsen and The Master Builder
Heinrich von Kleist
Art and Morality
Abolition of the Death Sentence

Onstage with Wedekind

*Introducing Colleagues and
Contemporaries of Frank Wedekind*

THEATER

Anton Chekhov, Russian playwright
Gerhart Hauptmann, German dramatist
Eugene O'Neill, American playwright
Luigi Pirandello, Italian dramatist
Arthur Schnitzler, Austrian dramatist
George Bernard Shaw, Irish playwright
Johan August Strindberg, Swedish playwright
Oscar Wilde, Irish playwright

ARTS

Alban Berg, Austrian composer
Gustav Klimt, Austrian painter
Gustav Mahler, Austrian composer
Edvard Munch, Norwegian painter
Auguste Rodin, French sculptor
Richard Strauss, German composer
Vincent van Gogh, Dutch painter
Richard Wagner, German composer

FILM

Thomas Edison, American inventor
William Kennedy Laurie Dickson, American inventor of celluloid strip
Louis Aimé Augustin Le Prince, French inventor

This section lists contemporaries whom the playwright may or may not have known.

Auguste and Louis Lumiere, French filmmakers
Georges Melies, French filmmaker
Eadweard Muybridge, English photographer
Robert W. Paul, English inventor of film projector
Edwin S. Porter, American filmmaker

POLITICS/MILITARY

Otto von Bismarck, German-Prussian statesman
Alfred Dreyfus, French army officer
Archduke Franz Ferdinand, Austro-Hungarian archduke
Napoleon III, French ruler
Nicholas II, last Russian czar
Theodore Roosevelt, American president
Queen Victoria, English monarch
Wilhelm II, German kaiser and king of Prussia

SCIENCE

Charles Darwin, English naturalist
Albert Einstein, German theoretical physicist
Sigmund Freud, Austrian physician and neurologist
Carl Jung, Swiss psychologist
Richard von Krafft-Ebing, Austro-German sexologist and
     psychiatrist
Walther Hermann Nernst, German physical chemist and
     physicist
Max Weber, German economist and sociologist
Orville and Wilbur Wright, American inventors

LITERATURE

Gustave Flaubert, French novelist
Edmond de Goncourt, French critic and diarist
Henry James, American novelist
Guy de Maupassant, French writer
Rainer Maria Rilke, Austro-German poet and dramatist
Arthur Rimbaud, French poet

Leo Tolstoy, Russian writer
Emile Zola, French writer

RELIGION/PHILOSOPHY

Karl Marx, German socialist philosopher
William James, American philosophy and psychologist
Friedrich Nietzsche, German philosopher, poet, and critic
Edmund Husserl, German philosopher of consciousness
Émile Durkheim, French philosopher and sociologist
Benedetto Croce, Italian philosopher of history and anti-Fascist
George Santayana, Spanish-American philosopher, essayist,
     poet, and novelist
Oswald Spengler, German philosopher of history

SPORTS

Baron de Coubertin, French founder of the modern Olympics
W. G. Grace, British cricketer
Tom Morris, Scottish golfer
James Naismith, Canadian-American coach and inventor of
     basketball
Spencer Gore, English cricketer and first tennis player to win
     a Wimbledon match
James Moore, English bicycle racer

INDUSTRY/BUSINESS

Karl Benz, German automotive engineer
George Eastman, American inventor
Henry Ford, American industrialist
William Randolph Hearst, American publisher
Gustav Krupp, German industrialist
Alfred Nobel, Swedish arms manufacturer
George Pullman, American industrialist
Henry Royce, British industrialist

WEDEKIND

in an
hour

OVERVIEW

Benjamin Franklin "Frank" Wedekind (1864–1918) lived one of the
most colorful and contradictory lives of modern times. A man uprooted
from childhood, he wandered the world in the company of adventurers,
libertines, and underground figures of mystery and intrigue. He was a
social reformer and addressed in his plays many of the struggles and
failings of the patriarchal, sexually inhibited Victorian culture of his
time. He has been called one of the major figures in modern drama for
his influence in breaking up the triteness of neo-Romanticism and the
stolidity of Naturalism.

Wedekind was a total anti-Naturalist, and his plays gain much of
their power from their bigger-than-life, grotesque, and often savagely
caricatured characters and situations. His plays were instrumental in
sweeping away the cobwebs and backwardness of theatrical conventions. In many ways, he is the link between the brilliant early-
nineteenth-century German playwright Georg Büchner and the later
avant-gardists, from Beckett to Ionesco and beyond. He was a vital

---

This is the core of the book. The essay places the playwright in the context of his or her world and analyzes the influences
and inspirations within that world.

forerunner of the subjective, uninhibited, and psychologically fragmented movement of Expressionism, and he is regarded as a direct influence on the mid-twentieth-century Theater of the Absurd.

MORALITY DIVIDED

Wedekind was the first to lash out against the hypocrisy of the middle class in the last decade of the nineteenth century — a society under the pall of sexual repression, a world in which one thing was preached and another was desired. He is rightly called the prophet of sexuality in modern drama. Society's antagonism toward the power of sex is the motivating force in his work.

Though he championed sexual liberation and the expression of repressed parts of the self, Wedekind was, nevertheless, a moralist. In his work, he demonstrates not just the freedom and power of sexuality, but the tragedy inherent in its destructiveness: This tragedy is seen in the death of many of his characters. Sex, he seems to say, is its own worst enemy.

Middle-class oppression was always with him, nagging and eating away at his conscience. Like the triumphant but tormented men of the Renaissance or his fellow countryman Johannes Faustus, Wedekind was torn between two divergent views: the new morality of sexual freedom and liberation versus conventional middle-class morality. One impelled him to express himself; the other fought this impulse and was his eternal torment.

A WANDERING FAMILY

Wedekind's father, Friedrich Wilhelm Wedekind, was a German liberal and a supporter of the 1848 revolution. A doctor, he wanted to establish an orthopedic clinic, but after a short time as a practical physician, he migrated to Constantinople, joined the Turkish service, and traveled with various expeditions to the Tigris and Euphrates

Rivers. Three years later, his father went from Palermo to Rome, a city he found so agreeable that he remained there until autumn 1847.

Disenchanted with the revolution of 1848 in its attempts at democratic action, Wedekind's father traveled to North America, where he made a fortune in land speculation and settled as a doctor in San Francisco. There he met and married Emilie Kammerer, a Hungarian-born actress and singer almost half his age from the local German-speaking theater. Two years later, in 1864, they returned to Europe, initially for a visit but ultimately to remain. It was in Hanover, Germany, that their second child, Frank — named Benjamin Franklin in honor of the land of freedom that had embraced them — was born on July 24, 1864.

Wedekind's father, who was independently wealthy, retired from his medical practice and gave himself over to politics. His disgust with Bismarck and his new Reich drove the Wedekind family to Switzerland in 1872, where they bought a castle, Schloss Lenzburg, in Canton Aargau.

Wedekind and his brother Armin lived a happy childhood in Switzerland; Wedekind was deeply committed to both his parents despite the frequent violent arguments between them, which he recalls in his diaries. Because of the family's liberal tendencies, the Wedekind children were tutored privately and in boarding schools. Wedekind's parents wanted him to become a lawyer, but he convinced his father to let him take a semester of literature and art courses. He attended the University of Lausanne and majored in German philology and French literature. In 1884, he and his brother went to Munich, a city that was to become central to most of Wedekind's life.

THE NATURALISTS

In 1886, Wedekind worked as a publicity agent for Maggi, a Swiss soup company near Zurich. That year he met the young Socialist-Naturalist group of writers known as Young Germany (Junges Deutschland), which included Gerhart Hauptmann, a famous

Naturalist playwright. Yet Wedekind had no leanings, even at that early age, toward what he perceived to be the dull and photographic observation that was the religion of the Naturalists. He was more interested in the mysterious underworld, with adventurers, drifters and artists, asocial types, and children, and he populated his plays with these characters.

His relationship with Hauptmann ended when Hauptmann broke a personal confidence. Wedekind had told Hauptmann about his parents' unhappy relationship and its effect on his childhood, and Hauptmann worked this information into his play *The Coming of Peace (Das Friedensfest)*. Wedekind retaliated with a satiric comedy, *Children and Fools (Kinder und Narren;* later retitled *The World of Youth [Die junge Welt]*), in which he ridiculed the photographic realism of the Naturalists.

Hauptmann introduced Wedekind to the work of Georg Büchner, the long-neglected and only recently rediscovered early-nineteenth-century playwright and revolutionary, who was a key influence on Wedekind's playwriting. Wedekind found the style of his future work in Büchner's plays: fragmented dialogue; frenetic, episodic scenes; a distortion of natural phenomena that moved the audience's focus to the emotional center of what was being conveyed; and the modern technique of isolation, with characters talking past rather than at one another.

Wedekind left Zurich to spend six months wandering from country to country with Herzog, a circus troupe, an entertainment he dearly loved. He visited London, Paris, Munich, Leipzig, Berlin, Silesia, Switzerland, Austria, and Southern Germany, where he wrote his first short sketches and stories. He frequently lived the life of the vagrants he identified with — the outsiders, the rejected, the socially reprehensible, the outcasts.

OUTSIDE INFLUENCES

As a man of the modern world, a man who gave expression to the modern world as few others of his time did (many have said, rightly, that he gave birth to modern theater), Wedekind had no superiors — at least, not in the arts. Outside the arts, he can be linked to a group of pioneers whose contribution to the modern world helped define it and its problems.

Social, scientific, economic, and musical revolutions were rocking nineteenth-century society. The year 1859 alone saw the appearance of three works that changed the world as Wedekind knew it: Charles Darwin's *On the Origin of Species*, Karl Marx's *Critique of Political Economy*, and Richard Wagner's *Tristan und Isolde*. Wagner's opera was, in its own way, a profound study in eroticism never before encountered. In 1886, Krafft-Ebing published *Psychopathia Sexualis*, his study of sexual perversions.

Of the pioneers of his time — and there were many more — the three of greatest importance to Wedekind were Marx, Friedrich Nietzsche, and Sigmund Freud, who put forward the possibility that Victorian neurosis could be traced to excessive sexual repression. What this group of groundbreakers had in common was a desire to achieve a freer, more natural, and more honest society. In studies such as *A General Introduction to Psychoanalysis*, *Beyond the Pleasure Principle*, and *Civilization and Its Discontents*, Freud laid bare what civilization had systematically concealed. He revealed what he believed to be the true nature of existence: the natural, instinctual life force, including sexuality. As Herbert Marcuse sums up in *Eros and Civilization*, "Civilization is based on the permanent subjugation of the human instincts."

Wedekind, like Freud, was committed to recovering the joy and freedom in life. In his search for civilization's liberation, Wedekind joined both Marx and Nietzsche, archenemies of the middle class and its self-complacency and inhibition. These two challenged society from opposite quarters, writes H. F. Garten in his book *Modern*

German Drama: "[Marx] stood for the revolutionary overthrow of bourgeois society, and its replacement by an entirely new social order; [Nietzsche's views] entailed a 'revaluation of all values,' challenging the moral standards on which the middle classes were founded, and setting up the image of the strong and independent individual; the first was collective and materialistic, the second individualistic and spiritual." There are aspects of both these views in Wedekind.

Wedekind was especially in agreement with Freud in the belief that the only way forward to a more natural, healthier life and society was to acknowledge our biological instincts. Freud called it the id, that part of the psyche regarded as the source of instinctual drive and psychic energy, dominated by pleasure and irrational wishing.

ART THAT CHANGES THE WORLD

Wedekind's life was not easy. The first forty years of his fifty-four years were, as one critic observes, "one continuous battle with the world." The arts of the nineteenth century did not lazily accept life as it was; theater's aim was to change the world, free it of its problems — particularly in regard to social issues. Naturalism, which originated in France and was championed by writers such as Émile Zola, Gustav Flaubert, the Goncourt brothers, and Guy de Maupassant, was preeminent. Defined at length by Zola, Naturalism insisted that the artist (in whatever medium) should faithfully follow nature; realism was paramount. To achieve this end, scientific observation, objectivity, and precision should be applied. Idealization and value judgments were to be avoided, whereas the repulsive side of life was not to be avoided. It was a philosophy of art that developed out of the mid-nineteenth-century revolution in science and political philosophy led by Darwin and Marx.

Though Wedekind fought Naturalism vigorously through his difficult and contentious life, he didn't lack concern for pressing social issues; he simply saw their remedy elsewhere. For Wedekind, Freud and Nietzsche were united by a single principle, which Wedekind fervently believed in: The resolution to society's problems lay within, not without, as the Naturalists believed.

VICTORIA AND THE WORLD VERSUS EROS

Wedekind lived during the Victorian Age (1837–1901), a socially repressive, sexually inhibited era. Wedekind believed, like Freud, that man's salvation lay in the liberation of primitive instincts from social conditioning. He believed that the psychic energy of man needed to be redirected. No longer should it be employed in the exhausting process of rejecting life; rather, it should accept all of life, including that basic primitive reality Freud termed the Pleasure Principle.

Wedekind's self-proclaimed mission was to reintroduce the world to what he called Eros. The developing discipline of psychology was also attempting to resurrect the sexual instinct, but it had a broader meaning for Wedekind. Eros brought with it, he was convinced, a unique spirituality. Eros was sacred, the oldest of the gods of antiquity, who precedes all things and rules all things. If Eros returned as part of everyday life, Wedekind believed, it would shake off the social repression of not only the Victorian world but thousands of years of civilization.

Wedekind had grown up in an atmosphere where anything could be discussed and had been exposed to liberal viewpoints on society, politics, and sex. His liberal upbringing set him at odds from the start with the Victorian way of life. He advocated the innate morality of the flesh, which was seen as unbridled *immorality* by those who subscribed to convention. His works were seen as sexual and scandalous, an image strengthened — even consciously created — by his public and private life. "He loved to play the Bohemian," writes Sol Gittleman in *Frank Wedekind*, ". . .[he] delighted in associating with the demimonde of forgers, circus people, and prostitutes, and at a time when his plays were receiving scant attention, his name was constantly exposed to the public through assorted trials, litigations, and numerous confrontations with the censors."

Gittleman makes a shrewd distinction between Freud's and Wedekind's vulnerability. Though they were saying the same thing regarding repression and the need to liberate the instincts to cure the sickness of mankind, Freud was shielded by his status as the detached scientist. Freud caused a stir, to be sure, but nothing compared with what Wedekind was forced to face. Wedekind was accused of being a pornographer and struggled his entire life to clear his name. What he viewed as a path to freedom was seen as obscene and heretical, a threat to society — and that society responded to his ideas with unprecedented, vicious defamation. "[It appeared as if] civilization had to defend itself against the specter of a world which could be free," comments Marcuse.

For all the passion that Wedekind exerted in his search for a non-repressive civilization, he — along with Freud — eventually came to the realization that such a civilization was impossible. Eros, the instinctual life force that was to bring liberation, could not stand up to thousands of years of social conditioning.

It took some time, however, for this reality to mature in Wedekind's understanding. In his earliest play, *The Quick Sketch Artist*, written in 1886, are some of the stylistic aspects that came to be associated with Wedekind, but no hint of the search for the Eros that was to be society's salvation. His first theatrical investigation of sexuality came the following year, 1887, in another early work, *Elin's Awakening (Elins Erweckung)*, of which there is only an unfinished fragment.

ELIN'S AWAKENING

Elin is a theology student whose first sermon is scheduled for Easter Sunday, but all is not well with him. He has begun to doubt his own spirituality. He is plagued by certain feelings, and he confesses the "impurity" of his dreams and thoughts to an objective and impartial friend, a young doctor. The friend assures him that what he is experiencing is both normal and desirable, that these are natural and instinctual urges. He also takes Elin to task for the moral dishonesty of his proposed Easter sermon. This exchange takes place in a cemetery (a somewhat heavy-handed symbol for society and civilization).

Elin and his doctor friend are interrupted when Ella, a young girl, enters. She is a prostitute fleeing from a well-heeled nobleman wielding a knife, Count Schweinitz. Ella, whose name means "light," embodies what Elin and his friend have been discussing. We see her power and independence when she defends herself with the statement: "You seem to think that because I survive from day to day with the aid of my naked body you can treat me as a dog. But I tell you that I am no more your property than you are a — a pillar of virtue!"

Written when Wedekind was twenty-two years old, the play is almost amusingly melodramatic and heavy-handed in its symbolism; an ardent anti-Naturalist, he was testing his wings as a playwright. But in this play, Wedekind expresses for the first time what will be his life's work in the theater. Ella is a major step, representing sexual emancipation; someone who has risen above society's damning judgment of her and her profession. She rejoices in sex because she sees its spiritual and transformative nature, the very aspects that Count Schweinitz and the society he represents have been conditioned not to see. She is the female deliverer from the repressive traditions of civilization. In doing so, she becomes nothing less than noble, while the nobleman Count Schweinitz is shown to be what his name signifies: a pig.

The cemetery scene represents an internal dialogue between the dual aspects of its author: one side caught in society's trap (Elin), and the other, revolutionary aspect (the doctor friend) trying to liberate it. Count Schweinitz threatening the life of Ella is a physical manifestation of Elin's "societal" problem.

Wedekind, in making Elin a student of theology, points out unequivocally how religion, through its basic fear and hatred of sex, creates guilt. But Elin, as the title foretold, has been awakened. He has seen the light. Ella's self-defense against Schweinitz is made possible by the transformation that has taken place in Elin through the discussion with his revolutionary, objective aspect, the "healing" doctor friend. The scene ends with Elin's rebirth, his flight with Ella from that place of the dead that is a symbol for society as Wedekind saw it.

What's in a Name?

Just as Ella's name implies enlightenment, wisdom, exaltation, and truth, Elin also means "light." Elin is a Superman, a Zarathustra who is a follower of Zoroaster, the god of creation, goodness, and light.

Wedekind's generic name for Ella is *das Freudenmädchen*, which is the German term for a prostitute or, more quaintly, "a woman of easy virtue." But the exact translation of *Freudenmädchen* is "daughter of joy." It is likely Wedekind knew perfectly well what he was doing when he called her that. Ella openly and proudly admits to being one who uses her body to get on in life; her uninhibited calling is spiritual because it is honest. No longer is "joy" a euphemism for sex as a degrading act, but it instead expresses the transcendent, innate spirituality of sex. Ella's sacredness can be equated with Goethe's archetypal Eternal Feminine that concludes his *Faust*, the feminine principle of nature that leads us to transcendence.

The Threat of Eros

Count Schweinitz, that pig of a man, will become a common dramatic type in Wedekind's work. He is the rigid, controlling counterpart to Eros' easy, flowing eroticism. He represents the status quo of the patriarchal system, a system that derives its dominance from wealth. He is *Homo economicus*. Money is power and power is control — and control is financial as well as physical. Always keep the body in check (one's own and others'), says *Homo economicus*, for the body can upset the financial cart with too much emotional expenditure. When one of

Wedekind's money-grabber types comes into conflict with one of his morally or sexually liberated types, whose mission is to transform the perverted ethical structure of life, *Homo economicus* will strive mightily to destroy them and the Eros they represent.

Eros is a threat, writes John Maynard Keynes, in *Essays in Persuasion*, because if society's morals are no longer built on accumulating wealth, the love of money will "be recognized for what it is: a somewhat disgusting morbidity, one of those semi-criminal, semi-pathological propensities which one hands over with a shudder to the specialists in mental disease."

Homo economicus in Wedekind's work (and in reality, as Keynes indicates) protects himself from falling prey to Eros either by exterminating her, as Schweinitz attempts, or by delaying satisfaction. "I will have my cake," says *Homo economicus*, "just not today; tomorrow, maybe." The problem is that tomorrow never arrives, or when the rigid, dominating money-grabber does indulge in the sensual, it is on his terms exclusively, unbendingly. It's simply a way to blow off a little steam so he can get back to filling his purse and continuing his march toward power. It is not *Homo economicus* who is transformed by the spirituality of Eros, but Eros who is demoted to inferior status by *Homo economicus*. Eros is a commodity to be used, not a joyful spirit to become one with in the process of transformation and renewal.

Is Count Schweinitz *Homo economicus*? Yes, but there may be more to him than meets the eye.

The Mousetrap

Schweinitz, as a generic type, makes frequent appearances in Wedekind's work. He is there to criticize one particular constituency in society: the artists. In Wedekind's work, the figure he criticizes most is the artist: not the artist who is true to the cause of societal emancipation, but the artist who has sold out.

"Since the figure of the artist, the artistic hanger-on, and all the many habitués of the artistic world (speculators, angels, financiers, tired businessmen, etc.) are the most frequent characters in Wedekind's plays it is as well to understand why they are there," says Alan Best, in his brief but splendid volume *Frank Wedekind*. He proceeds to tell us why. Artists can't be full members of society; they are inevitably on the fringe and are often made to feel inferior and insecure. But they aren't free from society; they still need the society that they have supposedly rejected and that has rejected them. As Best points out, "For all their grand talk and condescension to the 'common mass' they are where they are because there is nowhere else for them to go, and since they long for a secure social position they attempt to reconstruct social conventions in their own actions and relationships."

To Wedekind, the world of the artist is a microcosm of society. It has all the taboos, hypocrisies, and conventions of the larger society, which was Wedekind's real target. By reducing the macrocosmic world of society to the more manageable microcosm of the artist, Wedekind could better illustrate and criticize social conventions to his middle-class audience. Since the larger society looked upon artists as inhabiting a world apart, Wedekind could be ruthless in his censure of the artistic community and not appear to be attacking society. Just as a mousetrap is a lure for the unsuspecting mouse, so the Wedekind play lures the unsuspecting audience. "Only when the bait is swallowed," continues Best, "and the artistic world self-righteously condemned" does the middle-class audience member realize that there is no difference between the artistic way of life presented onstage and his own life.

Best, in his insightful analysis of Schweinitz's artist type, notes that Wedekind's artists fail because they too carefully follow middle-class practices: "They are searching for happiness and a sense of personal freedom in which they may fully express their own personalities and 'be themselves.' Unfortunately, however, society has so distorted the standards of the individual that self-expression assumes the guise of self-assertion at the expense of someone else."

His characters think they can find happiness through superiority and imposing their will on others. Best notes that "[t]his is an all-pervasive attitude, Wedekind believes, but is particularly clear-cut in society's ambivalent, hypocritical and degrading attitude to sexual matters."

Wedekind's failed artists — first seen in Schweinitz and later in the guise of Dr. Goll and Dr. Schön in the Lulu plays — will appear often on his stage.

SPRING'S AWAKENING

Three years later, with three plays now behind him, Wedekind took stock of what he had learned as a playwright and set to work on what is generally considered his most satisfying and poetic dramatic work, *Spring's Awakening (Frühlings Erwachen)*. Begun in 1890 and completed at Easter 1891, this play won him lasting fame as a playwright and also enormous conflict with the world of middle-class morality.

Rather than looking around him for models to emulate, Wedekind looked back to the early part of the nineteenth century to two playwrights whose styles rejected Realism: Georg Büchner (1813–37) and Christian Dietrich Grabbe (1801–36). In their works, Wedekind found artists like himself who were not interested in showing life as it is; they preferred, instead, to give the artist's personal vision, which had little relationship to the existing status quo. As Gittleman notes, Wedekind ignored the dramatic rules of the two conventional schools of his time, Realism and Naturalism. He developed the "Wedekind Style," in which he mingled tragic scenes with hilarious farce. Gittleman writes: "Endless speeches mouthed by dehumanized marionettes are followed by the staccato dialogue of children-poets. Psychological and dramatic motivation disappears, as scene after scene races by in a whirling of dynamic tension." What Wedekind also took from Büchner (but from his own experience as well) was a profoundly pessimistic view of things, that humanity has created an unfeeling, dehumanized world.

Moral Cowardice and All That

Spring's Awakening, labeled by its author "a tragedy of childhood," is the story of adolescence, when life is still mysterious, frightening, and wonderful, and confusion and elation are intermingled. The play focuses on three adolescents: the sexually frustrated and curious Moritz Stiefel; Melchior Gabor, Moritz's best friend, who is attacked by his parents and teachers for attempting to educate Moritz about sex; and Wendla Bergmann, a girl with no knowledge of the facts of reproduction who becomes pregnant by Melchior.

The underlying theme of the play is the opposition the children encounter from their elders just when they need openness and understanding, and how the way the adults treat them will determine their future course. Wedekind's children in the play are naïve; and it is from this naïveté that much of the play's beauty and strength derive.

The adolescents are caught up in the confusion that accompanies sexual awakening, questions concerning the nature of love and conception. Wedekind shows the wall erected by parents and teachers against responding to these perfectly normal concerns. The moral cowardice of the adult world that Wedekind criticizes results in Wendla's pregnancy, as well as her death at the hands of an abortionist brought in by her mother. The refusal of Wendla's mother to answer her questions about sex and reproduction has led to Wendla's pregnancy. School and teacher, too, come under fire; Wedekind typifies the latter as an overbearing, closed-minded, unfeeling example of bureaucratic machinery.

Mortiz's parents refuse to answer his questions about sexuality, so Melchior writes an essay on sexual intercourse for Moritz. Melchior's parents, the Gabors, who consider themselves towers of moral rectitude, send their son off to a reformatory as a punishment. They are, in effect, seeing to it that their son will become the hypocritical, well-oiled machine the middle-class bureaucracy is most comfortable with — assuming he survives in the first place. He will become part of the system, Wedekind implies, at the expense of his happiness and his very existence. It is Wedekind's most explicit statement regarding the sins of parents against their children: insistence on the death of natural instinct and desire.

Eros Reappears

It is in *Spring's Awakening* that Eros, first encountered in *Elin's Awakening*, makes its second appearance, this time in the character of Ilse. Just as the earlier Ella is defined by her name ("light"), so, too, is Ilse. Her name, derived from Hebrew, means "oath of God." She is a light-bringer, too, in the sense of enlightenment, wisdom, truth, and freedom — a task she boldly attempts to carry out. Ilse appears only twice in the play, just before Moritz's suicide at the end of Act Two and just after his burial.

Light and Dark

Moritz is afraid to tell his parents that he's doing poorly at school and frustrated by his failure to flee to America to avoid the issue entirely. He is also frustrated and confused by the promptings of his nascent sexuality, which his parents refuse even to discuss. All of this brings him to the overwhelming conclusion to end his life in suicide. At the close of Act Two, he has gone off into the woods to carry out his aim, and in a lengthy, highly poetic monologue, typical of the way Wedekind's children express themselves, he contemplates the unfairness of life — and yet wonders if there isn't something that can make it bearable. He finds himself in a no-win situation. He wants what he suspects is life's greatest gift, Eros, and yet he is afraid because the fear of Eros has been drummed into him.

Just when he is closest to giving into his fantasy of death by suicide, Ilse, as Eros, enters, "her clothes torn and with a bright kerchief around her head." She playfully grabs Moritz from behind by his shoulders, surprising him and rousing him from his seductive contemplation of death.

Ilse is a former schoolmate who, as Gittleman describes her, "has broken from the vapid atmosphere of her home and is currently leading a wild, uninhibited existence in the midst of a large number of male admirers." Ilse is sensual yet innocent and full of the joy of life. Her male admirers are sold-out artists who, Gittleman notes, "do not necessarily appreciate her inner beauty but who lust after her nonetheless."

Ilse realizes her superiority over these artists of the Wedekind world — grotesque, exaggerated types who are proxies for the middle-class world Wedekind is criticizing. "I've stuck kind of close to them actually," says Ilse of her band of admirers. "Nohl's a pig, Pandinsky's a monkey, Oikonomopulos' a camel, and then there's all the rest — but that's why I love them, and I wouldn't need another soul even if the world was made up of angels and millionaires!"

Ilse is utterly free, uninhibited, and everything that Moritz and his fellow adolescents are not — or, rather, not allowed to be. Ilse is as innocent as Moritz and his friends, except that the innocence of the other adolescents is enforced, whereas that of Ilse/Eros is based solely in her freedom from guilt and fear.

She tells Moritz about her ribald adventures in town over the last four days with an air of naturalness and joy that indicates how organic and free-flowing life is for her. She notices Moritz's strange behavior and asks him whether he has a hangover — which, of course, is unlikely. But he grasps the opportunity to drag himself out of his despondency by inventing an obviously foolish story of late-night partying to ease the sense of inferiority he feels as he measures his life against Ilse's heroically won freedom.

There is a moment of profound sadness when Ilse invites Moritz to come with her, and Moritz declines. He is faced with the grotesque contrast of his desperate fantasy with the reality of Ilse's uninhibited life. Ilse, despite the meaning of her name, is unable to bring light to

Moritz and his condition. Wedekind suggests why in his choice of the name Moritz, which translates as "he who is dark." It is tantamount to saying that there is no hope for him, nor was there ever, given the society he was born into.

Left alone, Moritz vacillates between living and dying, and finally kills himself.

Life in a Closed System

The four scenes that follow Moritz's suicide are pinnacles in Wedekind's work. Their condemnation of the adult world is so lethal as to banish all objectivity; the adult roles are caricatures carried to their cruel grotesque limits.

The first of these scenes takes place in the faculty room at the school. The teachers have been called together to consider the guilt of Moritz's best friend, Melchior, in the former's death, Melchior having written and illustrated for his friend's instruction an essay titled "Copulation." This essay was found among Moritz's effects and brought to the attention of the school authorities by his parents.

It is a scene of such idiocy, chaos, and distortion that it anticipates Dada and Surrealism by a quarter century. Into the mouths of these teachers, Wedekind puts, as Gittleman observes, "the most colossal inanities which, in themselves, argued against identifying these puppets as human beings." Just as the language of the children is lyrical in its innocence, the teachers' words are bloated, pompous, and absurd, as absurd as the names Wedekind has given them: Sunstroke, Puppylove, Bonebreaker, Barebelly, Stutterer, and Flyswatter, to name only a few in translation. With the future life of one of their students at stake, they no sooner get underway in their consideration of Melchior's case than they veer off into the unrelated and idiotic topic of whether or not to open a window in the room, a conversation they undertake with ludicrous seriousness.

When Melchior is brought into the room, the circus idiocy stops, and the atmosphere becomes intense and accusatory. Melchior is given no opportunity to defend himself. It would not be too much to say that the scene becomes a nightmare. As Gittleman has it, "Melchior's efforts at reason are futile in the face of society's irrational attack." He just manages to say that what he wrote is a very well known fact and asks where there is one offense against decency. But he is abruptly cut off, and Headmaster Sonnenstich tells him that he has no respect for either the faculty or man's shame "when faced with the moral order of the universe." The moral order of the universe is a closed system to these pedants. There is only one answer to any given question, and that answer is theirs.

Grotesque World versus Angelic Honesty

From the narrow, claustrophobic containment of that windowless faculty room and the insane and brutal immorality of its system of justice, we are swept immediately into a larger, more expansive, social context. The scene is Moritz's burial in the cemetery. It is pouring rain. Pastor Kahlbauch (Barebelly) stands at the foot of the open grave. Present are Moritz's father, Rentier Stiefel; a friend of his, Ziegenmelker (Goatmilker); and Uncle Probst. Of the faculty only Headmaster Sonnenstich (Sunstroke) and Professor Knochenbruch (Bonebreaker) are in attendance. Farther off we see Moritz's male school friends, and farther off still are Ilse and Martha, a schoolgirl.

Muted though this scene may be, it is no less grotesque. Here we are presented with another set of gross caricatures. Those gathered vehemently proclaim Moritz's hopeless depravity, his "serious offense" against moral order, and his unfair treatment of his parents. "He was no son of mine!" Rentier exclaims repeatedly. The adults console Rentier understandingly and quickly hurry off to get out of the rain and cold. There is little feeling for the life lost, except as it applies to the morals and structure of society.

— that there are no words to describe it. She must love
Wendla, in a way that at your age you could never love
o now you know.

's impossible," cries Wendla, referring to the earlier scene in a
ith Melchior. "We were lying there — I never loved anyone
rld except you, Mother."

vhich the mother responds: "How could I tell a fourteen-year-
uch things? I'd rather believe the sun could fall from the sky! I
me to you as my mother did to me. — We must trust in the
of God, Wendla; we must trust in His mercy and do our part!"
scene ends with a knock offstage, the opening of the door,
ntrance of Mother Schmidt, a local abortionist. The impli-
(just as in the case of the Gabors) that the Bergmanns' social
would be jeopardized if the pregnancy and birth were to go
Social respectability wins the day again, this time at the cost
la's life.

y's Pliers

e accusatory strokes delivered against the adult world, the
nate scene of the play is one of natural curiosity, joy, and
y of the Eros foremost in the mind of the author. Two of
male friends, Hans and Ernst, pursue each other, scarcely
g what it is they are after and finally express themselves in a
xual love scene of great delicacy, beauty, and humor. Yet, they
ht in the trap of their society, and they instinctively protect
ves from their confusion and isolation by taking refuge in the
tional" view of the future in which they see themselves as self-
ng, law-abiding, heterosexual bourgeois pillars of society,
hen they think back on "a night like this," will only laugh.

Wolfgang Kayser, in *The Grotesque in Art and Literature*, comments on Wedekind's treatment of the adult world in this scene:
"The caricatural distortion soon rises above the level of satire,
makes itself independent, and transforms human beings into rigid,
mechanically operated puppets. This arbitrary distortion, no longer
prompted by the satiric impulse, determines the outward appearance
of the characters, as well as their movements, thoughts, and
language."

After the adults leave, the boys gather around the open grave.
The rain has let up. From the gruesome, condemnatory world of the
adults, with their role playing and masks of social convention, we
suddenly find ourselves in a world in which role playing has no part:
the honest, open, lyrical, maskless world of the child. Moritz's friends
discuss his appearance at death, the five marks he still owes one of
them on a bet, his schoolwork and theirs. Within seconds of the
adults' departure, we hear phrases like "poor little dumbbell" and
"angelic honesty." The self-referential, egocentric adult world has
been replaced by the honest, simple, naïve world of childhood. Not
everything these children say is what would be called politically
correct today, but at least they are honest, albeit occasionally
unintentionally insensitive.

The boys depart, and Wedekind brings forward Ilse and the
young schoolgirl Martha, and through them he offers an even more
compassionate scene of youthful human concern free of solipsism.
True, Ilse wears a mask in her life of freedom, but it is one — multiple
ones, even — she chooses rather than one imposed by society or
convention. As she freely and joyfully admits in her conversation with
Moritz, she willingly dons a different mask for each role she chooses to
play for her artist friends and lovers, a mask she can change or remove
at will. Elizabeth Boa notes in *The Sexual Circus: Wedekind's Theatre of
Subversion* that her conscious choice of role within society enables her
to see through the masks of others.

Ilse shows Martha the pistol Moritz killed himself with, saying she intends to keep it as a "remembrance," and she vows to keep bringing fresh flowers — forget-me-nots — to Moritz's grave.

The Web of Social Behavior

The third scene is a discussion between Melchior's parents on what to do with their son. Mr. Gabor condemns him as "spiritually corrupt" and "rotten to the core" and says he must be sent to the reformatory, which "emphasizes the development of Christian thought and feeling." Previously, Mrs. Gabor was shown to be an ideal mother. Here, she roundly defends Melchior against her unfeeling husband and the faculty's unconscionable behavior in condemning her son, until her husband tells her that Melchior has gotten Wendla pregnant. At that point, Mrs. Gabor finally gives way and agrees to send Melchior to the reformatory. It is her husband's line that changes her mind: "It will be better for us," he says. The social disgrace of the incident is enormous and cannot be fought, and appearance takes precedence over personal relationships and understanding. "Despite herself she lacks the will and the strength to oppose her husband," writes Best. And society, he might have added.

Rivets in the Wall: Conformity at Any Cost

The fourth scene takes place in the reformatory and is a response to Melchior's father's statement that the institution "emphasizes the development of Christian thought and feeling." A group of young inmates are masturbating to see who can be the first to hit a coin in the middle of the circle. It is a scene that is shocking, brutal, and deliberately obscene for one reason only: to show society at large the dehumanizing institution it puts such faith in.

The reformatory warden describes his charges as "degenerates," but Wedekind suggests they are turned into degenerates by the system

that contains them. The warden's name, after all, the giant of Attica who seized travelers, tied them either stretched them or cut off their legs to make to secure conformity at any cost, reflected in his w who accompanies him. They enter in mid-conver:

> PROCRUSTES: True, the windows are on and there are thorn bushes planted bel degenerates know about thorn bushes! had one fall out of a skylight on us, and the bother of picking him up, carting hi ing him.
> LOCKSMITH: You say you want a wrought-
> PROCRUSTES: Wrought-iron, of course. A be fitted into the wall, it will have to be r

Melchior is an outsider to the group. He is of vulgarity of the situation if not by the act itself and It is clear he has not yet been dragged down to the cruelty, insensitivity, and indifference.

So Now You Know

The fifth and final accusatory scene takes place in V the Bergmann house. Pregnant, she is being treated character of a doctor named Brausepulver, which tr: Powder, a laxative. At the very end of the brief scene Wendla that she is pregnant, news that strains the gi comprehension. After all, when she asked her mothe come from, she was told by the prevaricating and m

> To have a child — a person must — must love married to — she must love him — as one can husband. She must love him so completely, wit

Eros/Wedekind: The Man in the Mask

The final scene of the play takes place in a graveyard. It is night, and the wind blows sky and earth. The ghost of Moritz, carrying under his arm the head he blew off, meets Melchior, who has just escaped from the reformatory and is in despair over the death of Wendla to the point that, were he not terrified of the possibility, he would kill himself. Moritz tries to lure him into taking his hand and joining him in death, but each time Melchior hesitates, wanting to but afraid. It is only when Melchior asks whether the dead can forget, and Moritz replies that the dead can do anything, that Melchior is sorely tempted — and stopped only by the entrance of the Man in the Mask.

There is a sense of déjà vu here, except that it is not illusory. It has happened before, at precisely the same moment — when a young person's decision to kill himself hangs in the balance. Eros has arrived again in the attempt to redeem a life.

In this graveyard scene, Wedekind reaches a degree of anti-Naturalism so great that scarcely a shred of reality remains — and he will continue that way in future works. Improbabilities will abound, psychology will be stood on its head, plot structure will frequently defy normal realistic expectation. If Ilse is the first manifestation of Eros in the play, her appearance is logical. But where does Eros' second manifestation come from? The impeccably dressed gentleman in formal attire and top hat? Played at the time, furthermore, by Wedekind himself? Remember that the ghost of Moritz appears carrying his head beneath his arm and engages in a lengthy scene with the living Melchior. Wedekind, the enemy of Naturalism, has reached a milestone — and he will never turn back.

The Poetry of Puberty

When one looks at the serious critical response to *Spring's Awakening* over the last century, one perceives that the play has the capacity to mean virtually anything one wants it to. "What is it all about?" asks W. B. Lewis in his study of Wedekind, *The Ironic Dissident*.

> Is it an allegory in which a character such as the Masked Gentleman has a meaning of its own? Is Wedekind in this way trying to explain or illustrate something? Or is it a problem play ("Tendenzstück"), a work with a message, written for the purpose of advancing a particular view? And with regard to the content, is the author providing a representation of puberty, advancing social criticism, seeking pedagogical enlightenment, or some combination thereof?

And the list goes on, proving that great literature has the capacity to arouse many conflicting opinions, some of which are as foolhardy as many others are perceptive. It doesn't matter whether the author himself issued a statement concerning his work's meaning, as Wedekind did regarding *Spring's Awakening*. "In a letter written in 1891 to an anonymous critic," writes Lewis, "Wedekind revealed his intention to depict poetically the phenomenon of puberty in order to facilitate more humane and rational views among parents and educators."

Which is not to say, of course, that it is *all* that the play is about.

Forget-Me-Nots

The best we can do in unraveling the fabric that Wedekind has woven is to say that the Man in the Mask is the spirit of life and leave it at that. That he is that vital spirit is evident from the fact that he rescues Melchior from death and, in wrapping him in his arms, repossesses him for the world of the living. One would like to add that he gives Melchior back to life, to beauty, to truth — to nature. Unfortunately that may not be the case, for the Man in the Mask tells Melchior quite clearly that he will be faced with "the enervating doubt about all things." In other words, what lies ahead for Melchior is a major battle to achieve a free existence. But at least he will have the chance.

So what is this new scheme of things? Given Wedekind's break from conventional new dramaturgy, what are we to say regarding Eros at the play's end? Eros, as Ilse, suffered a major setback in the attempt to rescue Moritz. But Eros is not defeated. Eros is still putting up a good fight. Wedekind the anti-Naturalist may be suggesting that this battle will be fought through Ilse's lovely act of planting forget-me-nots at Moritz's grave, plants she will take from the bank of the life-giving, fresh-flowing stream nearby. Perhaps that symbolic act will bear fruit even before the play is over. Perhaps Moritz and Melchior have now transcended their individual identities and become representative of a larger group. Is it possible to say that without Moritz's death and his subsequent attempt to lure Melchior, Melchior might not have had a chance at a better life? It's nice to think — however illogical — that Moritz has been useful in saving his friend, that Ilse's forget-me-nots have had their effect, and that Eros reappears once more in the guise of the impeccably dressed Man in the Mask.

Spring's Awakening is a tragedy of adolescence, the growth of the youthful characters checked and distorted by insensitive adults, caught in unthinking conformity to society. But, as Best points out, the tragic flaw in all Wedekind's characters is that they never grow up: "Their emotional development is checked by their childhood experiences and bourgeois upbringing."

LULU AND THE REIGN OF THE PHALLUS

The first of the "Lulu" plays, *Pandora's Box: A Monster Tragedy (Die Büchse der Pandora: Eine Monstretragödie)*, was written between 1892 and 1895. In this period, Wedekind struck up a love relationship with August Strindberg's second wife, Frieda, and traveled with her. She gave birth to their son, Frederich Strindberg, in 1897.

Wedekind worked on *Pandora's Box*, which he believed would never be either performed or published (at least in its original form) because of the moral outrage it would elicit. As expected, his Munich publisher refused the manuscript, but suggested that Wedekind revise the play, tone down the offending sections, and divide its monstrous length into two parts. This he did, titling the first half *Earth Spirit (Erdgeist)* and the second *Pandora's Box*.

In both the original and the revision, Wedekind, in total disregard of public convention and morality, lays bare the underside of life in a way that had never been seen onstage. In the character of Lulu, he presents a woman struggling against the odds of bourgeois male supremacy in a world in which the female was to be seen and not heard, where her role was to be a decorative motif in the life of the male.

Lulu sits still for no one. She moves forward with unflinching rapidity and resolve. She refuses to be caught up in the repressive demands of the social collective. She forges her own path. She is larger than life and something of an enigma: Lulu is all things and something different to every man she engages. She is fact, she is myth; she is corporeal, she is idea; she is realist, she is ideal.

Liberation is Lulu's goal, a goal she chases down with a vengeance — sexual liberation, social liberation, political liberation, personal liberation. Nobody owns her, nobody can handle her — though every man she encounters tries mightily to. Nobody knows who or what she is, and that's the way she wants it.

In one of the final scenes of the play, set in a dismal attic in a London slum where the characters will soon die, Schigolch (a mysterious figure who might or might not be Lulu's father), on his last legs, remarks: "I don't understand women." Lulu's fourth husband, Alwa, who will not survive the night, adds in despair: "I never understood them."

In all simplicity in her final degradation, Lulu replies: "I understand them." In that understanding she speaks for all women who have suffered the indignity of having lived — if that is the right word — in a male world.

Turning the Tables

With Lulu, Wedekind focuses his attention almost exclusively on the female for the first time — and subsequently on the battle for women's emancipation, one of the hottest topics of the day. The question for Wedekind now was: What is woman's role in society?

Up to this point in his work, Wedekind's definition of *das Freudenmädchen* had been, in Gittleman's words, "women born for pleasure who can find means to express their need only outside the normal channels of society." The major issue of contention between Wedekind and many women in the women's movement was their choice to "defeminize" themselves, to resign their womanhood in order to win equality with men. For Wedekind, a woman's greatest possession is her femininity — more directly, her sexual freedom. Her femaleness is her means to strike out against the inhuman restrictions of a patriarchal world and destroy it.

In the circuslike prologue to *Earth Spirit*, Lulu appears dressed as a gigantic serpent, equating woman with the animal world — "the wild and true and beautiful," as Wedekind describes her. Lulu (whose name also means "light," or "bringer of light") is the latest and the most extreme personification of Wedekind's Eros. Critics called her "fleshly lust personified," "woman in her most primitive form," "a mythic force incomprehensible to those who lust after her."

"Lulu was Wedekind's single most imposing symbol of his fight against civilization," writes Gittleman. She was everything civilized society was not, representing "mankind in his precivilized state, innocent and unpsychological, instinctive and supercharged with a strength which has become sublimated in modern society." By putting this primal force in the mainstream of civilization, Wedekind intended to create a conflict. Wedekind himself said, "she was created to stir up great disaster." Gittleman notes that "[f]or a time, anarchy runs loose on the stage. In this struggle between the unknown and the known, psychological meaning, accepted realities, and discursive thought are condemned, as Wedekind weaves the fabric of his theater of cruelty."

The Tragedy of Action

At the end of the third act of the original Monster Tragedy and at the end of *Earth Spirit*, Wedekind introduces an action that utterly changes Lulu's course. Up to this point, Lulu has been on a steady rise to her personal zenith as an untrammeled, instinctual being. But now she performs what may well be the first overt *action* in her life. She takes a life into her own hands and voluntarily extinguishes it, deliberately shooting and killing her third husband, Dr. Schön, who discovered the twelve-year-old Lulu selling flowers in a café late at night and took it upon himself to raise and educate her.

The murder is unpremeditated and somewhat justifiable. Schön is jealous of Lulu's many male admirers. In an ugly scene between Lulu and Schön, he castigates her loose behavior and various affairs. Revolver in hand, he vaguely threatens to kill her or her lovers, then gives the gun to her, instructing her to kill herself. He forces her to kneel down in front of him and tries to force her to turn the gun on herself. When he turns his back on her briefly, she immediately fires five shots into his back.

She kills him despite saying to herself that he is the only man she ever loved. This may be true, for Schön, in ruling Lulu with a meta-phoric whip, was the only man who ever stood up to her and gave her a hard time; for this she respected him. He made her what she is and gave her what she needed: security from societal ostracism.

In killing Schön, Lulu not only violates the law, but also her very way of being. The act makes her vulnerable to others, where before she was above the fray of everyday life. Her past innocence was founded on her inaction, but now she has suddenly, irrevocably — and unwittingly — turned the tables on herself. She is, for the first time, within reach of her society, the very thing she once controlled merely by *being*.

This tragic error propels Lulu beyond the limits of her existence. She is steadily, act by act, on the decline. She is exposed to being used by her fellows but is powerless any longer to use them. She might be blackmailed at any moment as a result of her escape from prison (where she was sent for the murder of Schön). Rodrigo, a seedy acrobat, is planning to turn her into a fabulous trapeze artist and become a wealthy man as a result; Casti-Piani, a count and procurer, is going to sell her to an expensive house of prostitution in Cairo. In the final act of the play, in the filthy London attic, damp with rain dripping in through the skylight, Schigolch and Alwa (her current husband and Schön's son, who is suffering from a venereal disease he has caught from Lulu) prostitute her services in order to bring in the little money they need to stay alive. In submitting, Lulu violates both her nature and her judgment, and this leads her to the only alternative: death.

Jack the Ripper Wins the Day

Wedekind's aim in the final act of the Monster Play and *Pandora's Box* is to summarize the rise and fall of Lulu as the divine embodiment of Eros. We see this when Countess Geschwitz enters with a full-length portrait of Lulu as Pierrot that she carries with her everywhere as a reminder of Lulu's former glory. The portrait has been ripped from the frame that once hung in the elegant salon of Schwarz, Lulu's second husband, and is now nailed to the wall of the ratty London attic in the Soho district where, in flight from the police, Lulu brings her customers. We see her service three bizarre examples of male: a mute customer who communicates only through gesture; a timid and sexually inexperienced Swiss academician who wants to try out sex in preparation for his imminent wedding night; and Kungu Poti, crown prince of an African state, who mortally wounds Alwa when the latter charges him in a jealous rage.

Lulu's final degradation in her decline comes in a scene of near unspeakable violence with Jack the Ripper, whom she has enticed to the attic. He rapes her in her room; she escapes into the main room, but Jack retrieves her and drags her back into her room, where he murders her and carves her vulva out, wrapping it in a newspaper as a memento of the occasion before killing Countess Geschwitz and departing.

Society has had its revenge on innocent, freedom-seeking Lulu, now degraded and powerless as a prostitute, writes Gittleman. "I can't make love on command," she says. Because she is untrue to her nature, her strength is gone, and she is "left completely disarmed before Jack . . . a horrible sexual variant of inhibited humanity." She could once have been a match for him, but she has lost her instinctual sexual power and become a common whore and so is annihilated. Lulu, Wedekind's most powerful embodiment of Eros in his entire body of work, was not up to the task of bringing civilization a revitalizing and freedom-oriented way of life and love, free of guilt, free of repression, free of the need to kill off its opposition in order to guarantee its security.

But perhaps Lulu failed not so much because of her inability but because civilization's defense system was so monumentally unshakable that not even a divine impulse could budge it. Consider the physical manifestation and reputation of Jack the Ripper, the force that destroys Lulu, the infamous, perverted, antisocial, pathological serial killer that Wedekind made the ultimate demonic victor of his saga. This choice of character shows the bleakness of Wedekind's outlook for the reformation and restitution of life as it should be lived.

On a personal note, Wedekind played Jack the Ripper himself. Mathilde (Tilly) Newes was Lulu. The two became involved and married in 1906. Their marriage was reportedly stormy. Wedekind was twenty years her senior, and frequently jealous of her — so jealous that she stopped taking other parts and only acted opposite her husband. They had two daughters, Anna Pamela, known as Pamela, and Fanny Kadidja, called Kadidja.

THE TENOR

With Eros temporarily fading from the scene after the Lulu plays, Wedekind took up issues begun a few years earlier. One of his most successful plays, *The Tenor (Die Kammersänger)*, is a farce about the man who works as opposed to the man who enjoys himself, a subject that occupied Wedekind on a number of occasions.

In this one-act, written in 1897, a famous Wagnerian singer, Gerardo, is on a tour of the provinces. He has just sung the role of Tannhäuser the night before, and he is now in his hotel room packing in order to catch a train to Brussels, where he will sing Tristan the following night. He asks not to be disturbed, but he is besieged, one by one, by three individuals who manage to find their way in. The first is a lovesick teenager, Miss Coeurne; the second an aged, white-haired, unknown opera composer, Professor Dühring; and the third the town's most ravishing young woman, Helen, with whom Gerardo had a brief affair during his stay.

Miss Coeurne is fairly easily dealt with; she is inexperienced but infatuated, and settles for an autographed photograph. The second interruption is considerably more complex. Dühring has composed many operas but has failed to have even one performed in over fifty years of work; he begs Gerardo to look at his score and give him a judgment. The battle between them continues at length, with many arguments engaged, the most significant being that Gerardo hasn't the time. He reminds Dühring over and over that he is an artist, that he has his career to think of, that he is contracted, that his manager will drop him if he does not catch the next train to Brussels to sing Tristan, that everything in his life depends on his fulfilling his contract. To which the pathetic Dühring, whose life is his art, who refuses to compromise his work with mediocrity, stands up to Gerardo with nothing less than genuine romantic passion — but to no avail. Nonetheless, he leaves with head held high, secure in his belief in himself as an artist.

While Dühring's life is his art, Gerardo's art is his life, which is to say no life, for it is duty-bound, contract-bound, the need-to-arrive-in-Brussels-on time-bound, impersonal. He is, in short, a slave to his art, and all for one thing — money. "Gerardo," observes Lewis, "can offer no help [to Dühring] since singing an unknown role would reduce his market value." Gerardo is interested in one thing only: the performance, not the music, for it is the performance by the star that determines economic success.

Things are no different in the scene with Helen, except that love is introduced into the equation. Helen dearly loves Gerardo. Unhappily — though wealthily — married, her only happiness, she insists, could be with Gerardo, and she will do anything to achieve that. As anticipated, Gerardo resorts endlessly to contract and duty and agent and arrival on time. In tandem, Dühring and Helen represent art and love respectively.

While there have been many pronouncements regarding the intention behind the play, the one that appears most Wedekindian has to do with *Homo economicus*, first encountered in Count Schweinitz of *Elin's Awakening* — the man who protects himself from falling prey to Eros by exterminating her or delaying satisfaction in order to keep the cash flowing in. Gerardo is such a man.

"For [the tenor] his art becomes a compensation for life," writes Lewis, "which no longer bears social significance." He is *Homo economicus*, who cancels out Eros, or merely dabbles in it and then departs without concern or commitment. In the end, Helen commits suicide. With Helen propped up in his arms, trying futilely to revive her, Gerardo still frets that he will be in breach of contract if he fails to arrive on time in Brussels. Unless, of course, he is apprehended by the police, which will at least give him an excuse. He looks for a policeman but doesn't find one, so off he rushes, letting Helen's body fall hard to the carpet, shouting as he runs: "I have to sing *Tristan* tomorrow in Brussels!"

HOMO ECONOMICUS IIN FULL ARMOR

The Lulu plays, too, have their parade of the *Homo economicus* — and a marvelous assortment they are, each with his different eccentricity, each serving as a counterforce to Lulu's life force. First there is Dr. Goll, an old, doting, probably impotent little physician — and wealthy, one must assume, given his lifestyle. Goll's counterforce is to keep Lulu a virtual prisoner, to control her every move. He uses her as a plaything, as if she were a mechanical doll that performs when wound up. He plays his violin and she dances, an occupation for which she has many costumes. He doesn't trust her to sit alone to have her portrait painted, but accompanies her and is lured away only by the prospect of seeing the ballerina Corticelli rehearse in his son Alwa's dance drama. Goll is so jealous of Lulu that he suspects her of infidelity when he returns to the painter's studio, and he collapses and succumbs to a heart attack.

Then there is the penniless Schwarz, the artist painting Lulu. His marriage to Lulu is arranged by her patron, Schön, almost as soon as Goll is dead. Schön becomes Schwarz's patron as well, bolstering him with wealth, seeking out commissions for him so he can provide for Lulu in proper fashion.

Just as with Goll, Lulu is highly protected by Schwarz. He can't rise from bed in the morning without anxiety that something will harm her, that an insect will bite her, that a mad dog will attack her. Lulu complains to Schön that Schwarz is like a child, he's naïve, he worships her — he's tedious, he's insufferable. When Schigolch, Lulu's mysterious father figure, suggests that she is too well off, her reply is: "Almost to the point of losing my mind." Her life, her being — her cosmic purpose, as Wedekind might put it — is thwarted. Just as with

Goll, but in quite a different way, Schwarz restricts her with near imbecilic worship. Lulu is a kept thing, a property to boost Schwarz's self-confidence. Once more, just as with the jealous Goll, Schwarz kills himself in despair when he suspects Lulu's infidelity.

Then there is Schön, who arranged both of Lulu's marriages. Why not marry her himself? After all, he discovered her when she was twelve, barefoot and selling flowers in cafés. He took her into his care, had her raised and educated. In every respect he has played her Pygmalion, and she is his to do with as he sees fit. The fittest thing he sees to do is to keep her in check, keep her married, keep her from interfering in his life and distracting him from his main purpose: acquiring wealth. He is *Homo economicus* in full armor. To him, Lulu is a property that he must handle as rationally, dispassionately, and with as brutal an intellectual rigor as he manages his financial empire.

"Throughout his plays, [Wedekind] parades a long line of social, economic, and sexual predatory types," says Gittleman, "robber barons of sex and society, who demonstrate a lust for power both financial and physical." Schön uses Lulu to show the degree of his power to domi-nate — physically as well as economically. Considering that the power of Lulu's life force is cosmic in Wedekind's understanding, Schön is taking on a Herculean task. Yet, these representatives of rational, economically oriented society inevitably win out.

But that inevitable triumph over Eros doesn't come without a fight. At the end of Act Three of *Earth Spirit*, Lulu wins an extra-ordinary battle of wills against Schön. In response to a reference Lulu makes to her attractive naked shoulders, Schön remarks: "That's why I married you." Lulu replies: "You didn't marry me." "What, then?" responds Schön. "I married *you*," says Lulu.

With her murder of Schön, Lulu begins her rapid decline because she opens herself up to being used by others, where previously she used people for her own ends. Lulu became vulnerable to legal pros-ecution, but in Jack the Ripper she is faced with a force more powerful even than the law. He and his brutal inhumanity is Wedekind's surrogate for "civilization-conditioned society," the evil, predatory beast that Wedekind always attacks. Jack the Ripper may not be *Homo economicus* in the traditional sense, but he is as powerful as the wealthiest financier because of the irresistible force he represents: the social collective. He carries out society's punishment of Lulu by carving out her vulva, a fitting revenge for Lulu as the Eros that would liberate society of sexual denial, repression, and guilt.

TURNING THE TABLES

In 1905, ten years after completing the Monster Tragedy (and eventually revising it), Wedekind returned to the subject of sex in *Death and Devil (Tod und Teufel)*, but with an unanticipated message.

At the end of the Monster Tragedy and *Pandora's Box*, we saw a pitiable Lulu defeated by a civilized world. In 1894, while still at work on the Monster Tragedy, Wedekind began writing *The Solar Spectrum (Das Sonnenspektrum)*, subtitled *An Idyll from Modern Life*. The play is an idealization of the prostitute and the bordello; it takes place in a garden of paradisiacal beauty, a place of freedom and contentment where lovely women meet men of extreme good manners and pedigree. That this play was in the works while the second half of the Monster Tragedy was being written is most odd. If nothing else, it demonstrates in a very dramatic way how Wedekind's mind and soul were divided. This division reappears in *Death and Devil*.

In *Death and Devil* we again see Count Casti-Piani, the procurer of *Pandora's Box* who proposed selling Lulu into prostitution but failed. Whether this is the same Casti-Piani is debated, but he certainly holds many of his earlier version's beliefs. In the new play, Casti-Piani, a trader of female slaves, is approached by Elfriede, a young woman — and a member of the International Society for the Suppression of White Female Slave Traffic — who deeply opposes him on all counts. Casti-Piani has a seemingly unshakeable belief in the exalted view of prostitution as woman's highest calling, but over the course of the play this is reversed.

In an attempt to convince Elfriede of the rightness of his belief, he arranges for them to overhear a conversation between one of his girls and a male customer. During the conversation, he learns the magnitude of his delusion and the evil he has wrought on the world. In his despair he shoots himself, saying: "I wish I'd put a bullet through my skull fifty years ago."

It is possible to say that Wedekind had no personal connection to *Death and the Devil*; but so often is his work demonstrably infused with autobiography that not to see it here is perhaps perverse.

VISIONS AND VENGEANCE

Perhaps the best way to describe Wedekind as a playwright is to call him a teacher. His aim from the start was to teach what he deeply believed to be good for society and to deliver his message not one jot less profoundly than his contemporaries Marx, Nietzsche, and Freud. He set out with a vision and a vengeance, and he bent the accepted, traditional rules of playwriting to meet his needs. He fractured structure. He rejected realism. He had no truck with psychology. His characters wear who and what they are on their sleeves; they are puppets who do the bidding of their maker. Wedekind created a theater based not on an illusion of reality, but on a vital social message.

Wedekind wrote plays nearly until the day he died in 1918 at the age of fifty-four. He was buried in Munich. Thousands of notables and Bohemians came to honor him. The work he turned out the last decade of the nineteenth century, 1890–1900, has lasted and had a major effect on virtually all new forms of theater that followed it — from Expressionism to Dada, Surrealism, the Epic Theater of Brecht, Frisch and Dürrenmatt, and the Theater of the Absurd.

In every sense, Wedekind was a social reformer. Like all social reformers, he met with social resistance. His work was censored, and he was kept in theatrical limbo for most of his productive life. It was only after his death, and after World War I, that his works came to be performed regularly. But even that lasted only a brief time, for Wedekind was not on the list of favorite sons of the Nazi party and performances of his plays were banned in Germany until the end of World War II. It was only then that his work was taken seriously and found viewers and readers.

The future seems bright for Wedekind's major plays, and the future can only benefit from their profound vision.

DRAMATIC MOMENTS

from the Major Plays

These short excerpts are from the playwright's major plays. They give a taste of the work of the playwright. Each has a short introduction in brackets that helps the reader understand the context of the excerpt. The excerpts, which are in chronological order, illustrate the main themes mentioned in the In an Hour essay.

from **Spring's Awakening** (1891)
from Act One, Scene 6

CHARACTERS

Ernst Roebel
Hans Rilow

[This three-act play chronicles the sexual awakening of twelve adolescents and how the adults mishandle their questions and explorations, with tragic results. In this scene, two young friends, Ernst and Hans, enjoy an innocent, peaceful moment together.]

A hillside vineyard. The sun is setting behind the mountains. The clear sound of bells floats up from the valley. Hans Rilow and Ernst Roebel are rolling around in the dry grass at the top of the vineyard beneath overhanging rocks.

ERNST: I think I overdid it.

HANS: Let's not be sad. — It's a pity the way time flies.

ERNST: You see them hanging there, but you just can't stuff another one down — and then tomorrow they're in the winepress.

HANS: Being tired is just as bad as being hungry.

ERNST: Oh, I just can't eat any more.

HANS: Just one more fat, shining, beautiful grape!

ERNST: My stomach can't stretch any farther.

HANS: If I bend down the shoot, it'll swing back and forth between our mouths. We won't even have to move. Come on, Ernst. We'll bite off the grapes and let the stalks swing back to the vines.

ERNST: Why do we make resolutions when all we do is break them?

HANS: And then there's the gorgeous fiery sky at sunset — and the evening bells — what more can I ask out of life?

ERNST: Sometimes I imagine myself a worthy pastor, with a motherly wife, a well-stocked library, and duties to perform and positions to hold in the community. For six days you meditate, and on the seventh you speak. And when you go for a walk, school children come up and shake hands with you. And when you get home you find the coffee steaming, and the cake is brought in, and girls bring apples to you through the garden gate. Can you imagine anything more wonderful, Hans?

HANS: I'm always thinking about half-closed eyes, parted lips, and Turkish draperies. I don't believe in suffering for love, and pity, and all that. Do you know why our parents go around looking so serious all the time? They're just trying to hide how stupid they are. I *know*. When I become a millionaire I'll build a monument to God. — Think of the future as a milk-pudding with sugar and cinnamon. One person spills it all and howls, and the other stirs it into a mess till he sweats. Why not just skim the cream off the top? Or don't you think we can learn how?

ERNST: Let's skim it off!

HANS: And what's left we'll throw to the chickens. — I've gotten out of more scrapes than I can even remember —

ERNST: Let's skim it off, Hans! — Why are you laughing?

HANS: Are you starting in again?

ERNST: Well, somebody has to.

HANS: Thirty years from now, when we think back on an evening like this, it might seem beautiful beyond words.

ERNST: Can it get that way by itself?

HANS: Why not?

ERNST: If a person were all alone, he could burst out crying —

HANS: Let's not be sad. *(Kisses Ernst on the mouth.)*

ERNST: *(Kisses him back.)* I left the house thinking I'd only talk to you and go right back home.

HANS: I was waiting for you. — Virtue isn't such a bad suit of clothes if you've got the body to wear it.

ERNST: It sure hangs loose on us though. — I could never have been happy if I hadn't met you. I love you, Hans, like I've never loved anyone before —

HANS: Let's not be sad! — When we think back on this in thirty years, we might even make fun of it all. But right now it's so beautiful — the mountains glowing in the sun, the grapes hanging down into our mouths, and the breezes stroking the rocks like a playful kitten —

****

from **Earth Spirit** (1895)
from Act Three

CHARACTERS

Alwa
Lulu
Schön

[Schön met Lulu when she was a twelve-year-old girl selling flowers on the street. He rescued her and has helped her become a successful performer. However, he consequently feels he owns her and often bullies and insults her. Here, she is unhappy about the prospect of dancing in front of Schön's fiancée.]

A theater dressing room. Lulu enters in a dancing costume.

ALWA: Did you faint?

LULU: Close the door.

ALWA: At least go back on stage.

LULU: Did you see him?

ALWA: Who?

LULU: With his fiancée?

ALWA: With his — *(To Schön, as he enters.)* You might have spared her that joke!

SCHÖN: What's the meaning of this? *(To Lulu.)* Don't you ever give up?

LULU: I feel like I've been whipped.

SCHÖN: *(After locking the door.)* As long as you are my responsibility — you will get on that stage and you will dance!

LULU: In front of your fiancée?

SCHÖN: In front of anyone I say! You are under contract! You are being paid a salary!

LULU: That's none of your business!

SCHÖN: You will dance in front of anyone who buys a ticket. Whom I choose to sit with in my box has nothing to do with your activities on that stage.

ALWA: Go back to your box! *(To Lulu.)* Would you mind telling me what I'm supposed to do? *(A knock at the door.)* The stage manager! *(Calling.)* I'll be there in a minute! *(To Lulu.)* I trust you won't force us to break off the performance!

SCHÖN: *(To Lulu.)* Get out on that stage!

LULU: Wait. I can't. I'm ill.

ALWA: Show business!

LULU: Start the next number. No one will know. I'll be there in five minutes. I'm too weak.

ALWA: But you'll dance?

LULU: I'll do my best.

ALWA: As badly as you like. *(At the repeated knocking.)* I'm coming! *(Goes off.)*

LULU: You're quite right putting me in my place. And what better way than making me dance in front of your fiancée. Thank you for reminding me of my position.

SCHÖN: *(Scornfully.)* Considering your origins, you're lucky a respectable audience will sit still for you.

LULU: Even when my shamelessness makes them uncertain where to look?

SCHÖN: Shamelessness? Don't be a fool. And don't make a necessity of virtue. Every shameless step you take is paid its weight in gold. A bravo and a boo mean the same thing to you. Your greatest triumph is nearly to drive a respectable girl from her seat. It's your single goal in life. But you'll never be a dancer as long as there is an iota of self-respect in you. The higher your shock value, the higher your rating.

LULU: I couldn't care less what people think of me. I don't want to be better than I am. I'm satisfied.

SCHÖN: *(Shocked.)* That's the first honest word I've heard out of you. You're corrupt!

LULU: Self-respect? It never occurred to me.

SCHÖN: *(Suddenly suspicious.)* None of your tricks.

LULU: Oh, God — I know what would have become of me if you hadn't saved me.

SCHÖN: Oh? Have you changed?

LULU: Not a bit.

SCHÖN: Yes, that's just like you.

LULU: *(Laughs.)* And I'm insanely happy.

SCHÖN: *(Spits out.)* Are you going to dance now?

LULU: *Any way* and in front of *anyone!*

SCHÖN: Then get out on that stage!

LULU: *(Pleading like a child.)* Just one more minute. Please. I can't stand yet. They'll ring.

SCHÖN: So this is what all my sacrifices for you have come to!

LULU: *(Ironically.)* So much for your ennobling influence.

SCHÖN: Spare me your witticisms.

LULU: The Prince was here.

SCHÖN: Well?

LULU: He's taking me to Africa.

SCHÖN: Africa?

LULU: Why not? You made me a dancer so someone could "whisk" me away, didn't you?

SCHÖN: But to Africa?!

LULU: You should have just let me faint and silently thanked your lucky stars.

SCHÖN: You didn't faint.

LULU: *(Contemptuously.)* You couldn't stand it out there any longer.

SCHÖN: I had to convince you of who you are and where you belong.

LULU: Were you worried I'd hurt myself?

SCHÖN: You're indestructible.

LULU: You know that, do you?

SCHÖN: *(In a burst of rage.)* Don't look at me like that!

LULU: No one's keeping you.

SCHÖN: I'll leave when the bell rings.

LULU: No. When you have the energy. What's happened to that fabled energy? You've been engaged for three years now. Get married! No one's stopping you. So don't blame it on me. You insisted I marry Dr. Goll; I married Dr. Goll. You insisted I marry the painter; I married the best of a bad bargain. You create artists. You are the patron of princes. Get married!

SCHÖN: *(Raging.)* Don't flatter yourself!

LULU: *(Exultant from here to the end of the scene.)* You have no idea how happy your anger makes me, and how proud I am to be humiliated by you. You degrade me as totally as a man can degrade a woman so you can ignore me all the more easily. But your every word to me has damaged you beyond repair. I see it in your face. Your self-control has almost run its course. Get out of here. For your innocent little fiancée's sake, leave me alone. Another minute and your mood will change and you'll find yourself in another scene that won't be as easy to justify.

SCHÖN: I'm not afraid of you. Not any more.

LULU: Of me? — Be afraid of yourself, why don't you? — I don't need you. Get out. Just don't blame me. I don't need to play games to destroy you. Your faith in my integrity is awesome. I'm not just a little tart to you, I'm a tart with a heart. But actually I'm neither. Your problem is that you *think* I am.

SCHÖN: *(Desperate.)* Don't tell me what to think! You've already destroyed two husbands. Marry the prince. Dance him to his destruction, too. I wash my hands of you. I know where the angel in you stops and where the devil begins. If I accept the world as it is, then it's the Creator who'll answer for it, not me. Life is no amusement for me.

LULU: And yet you make more demands on life than anyone. Tell me, which of us asks more out of life? You or I?

SCHÖN: Shut up! I don't know what I think. When I listen to you I stop thinking. I'll be married in a week. I beg the angel in you not to see me before then.

LULU: I'll bolt my doors.

SCHÖN: So pleased with yourself, are you? — God as my witness, I have never in my life cursed anyone as deeply as I curse you.

LULU: Because I'm base?

SCHÖN: Because you're depraved!

LULU: Ah, so then I *am* to blame! Delighted! How pure you must feel! A model of austerity, a paragon of unshakable principles. Otherwise how could you marry that insanely innocent girl?

SCHÖN: Do you want me to kill you?

LULU: *(Quickly.)* Anything to make you touch me. I wouldn't be in that child's shoes for a king's ransom. And yet she loves you as no one ever has.

SCHÖN: Monster! Stop it! Stop it!

LULU: Marry her! Then *she* can be miserable dancing in front of *me!*

SCHÖN: *(Raising his fist.)* God —

LULU: Beat me! Where's your whip? Hit my legs!

SCHÖN: *(Hands at his temples.)* I have to leave here! *(Rushes to the door, reflects, turns.)* Can't see her — like this — go home — why can't I die!

LULU: Try being a man. Take a good look at yourself. You have no conscience. No act is despicable enough for you. All you want is to make that poor girl's life miserable. Because she loves you. You conquer half the world. You do whatever you like. But inside you know. You know.

SCHÖN: *(Exhausted, collapses in the armchair, left.)* Stop!

LULU: You know you're too weak to tear yourself from me.

SCHÖN: *(Groaning.)* You're hurting me!

LULU: There are no words to tell you how happy I am! How happy!

SCHÖN: *(Moaning.)* I'm old — it's over —

LULU: Behold, the fearsome lion weeps! Go tell your fiancée the marvelous woman I am! And not one bit jealous!

SCHÖN: *(Sobs.)* The child! The innocent child!

LULU: So strong! So weak! Go to her. Please go. Go to your fiancée. I wouldn't wipe my feet on you.

SCHÖN: I *can't* —

LULU: Get out! Come back when you're strong!

SCHÖN: What can I *do*?

LULU: *(Rises; her cape remains on the chair. She sweeps the costumes on the center table to the side.)* Here's stationary —

SCHÖN: I can't write —

LULU: *(Standing erect behind him, leaning on the back of his chair.)* Write! "My dear Countess — "

SCHÖN: *(Hesitantly.)* I call her Adelaide —

LULU: *(Emphatically.)* "My dear Countess — "

SCHÖN: My death sentence —

LULU: "You must take back your promise of marriage. I cannot reconcile it — " *(As Schön puts down the pen and looks at her imploringly.)* Write! — "cannot reconcile it with my conscience to bind you to my miserable existence — "

SCHÖN: *(Writing.)* You're right. — You're right.

LULU: "I am not worthy — " *(As Schön again turns to her.)* Write! " — not worthy — not worthy of your love. For three years I have tried to tear myself away; but I haven't the strength. I write to you now at the side of the woman who masters me. You must forget me. — Dr. Ludwig Schön."

SCHÖN: *(Groaning aloud.)* God!

LULU: *(Half frightened.)* Weakling! *(With emphasis.)* "Dr. Ludwig Schön." — "P.S. Make no attempt to rescue me."

SCHÖN: Now — for the execution —

****

from **The Tenor** (1899)

CHARACTERS

> Helen Marova
> Gerardo
> Valet

[Gerardo, a Wagnerian singer, is on a tour in the provinces. He has just sung the role of the Tannhäuser and is in his hotel room packing, about to catch a train to Brussels. Though he has asked not to be disturbed, two people have managed to visit him, interrupting his packing: a lovesick teenager and an aging unknown composer. Now a third visitor comes, getting past the valet guarding the door: Helen Marova with whom Gerardo once had a brief affair.]

A luxurious hotel room.

HELEN: *(A radiant beauty, twenty years old, dressed in street clothes, with a muff, enters extremely excited.)* I suppose you thought he could keep me out of here! — Why else would he be standing down there guarding the door!

GERARDO: *(Has jumped up.)* Helen!

HELEN: You knew perfectly well you'd see me again!

VALET: *(In the doorway that she has left open, his hands at his cheeks.)* I did what I could, Mr. Gerardo, but the lady —

HELEN: Boxed your ears!

GERARDO: Helen!

HELEN: Am I to stand around and be insulted?!

GERARDO: *(To the Valet.)* You may go.

(The Valet exits.)

HELEN: *(Puts her muff on the chair.)* I can't live without you any longer. You will either take me with you or I shall go to my death.

GERARDO: Helen!

HELEN: I shall go to my death. You would be severing my very existence if you were to part from me! My mind and heart are no more. If I must experience another day like yesterday, without seeing you, then I shall never live through it. I haven't the strength. I beg of you, Oscar, take me with you! I beg of you, for my life's sake!

GERARDO: But I can't.

HELEN: You can if you want to. What do you mean, you can't? Leave me and you're the cause of my death. Those are no empty words. I'm not threatening you with them. They're the truth. I'm as certain of that as I now feel the beat of my own heart. I'm dead without you. And so you must take me with you. It's your duty as a human being. Even if only for a while.

GERARDO: On my word of honor, Helen, I can't. On my word of honor.

HELEN: But you must, Oscar, you must. Whether you want to or not, you must accept the consequence of your actions. Life is precious to me, and you and life are one. Take me with you, Oscar. Take me with you, unless you'd have my blood on your conscience.

GERARDO: Do you remember what I told you the first day I saw you in this very room?

HELEN: Yes! Yes! But what good is that to me now?

GERARDO: That sentiment must have no part of our relationship?

HELEN: What good is that to me now? I didn't know you then. I didn't know what a man could be like until I knew you. You knew that it would happen, you knew. Otherwise you'd never have made me promise not to make a scene at your departure. And what wouldn't I have promised you then if you'd asked me. That promise is my death. Leave me now and you've cheated me of my life.

GERARDO: I can't take you with me.

HELEN: My God, I knew before I came that you'd say that. I knew when I came. It stands to reason. You say that to every woman. And why should I be any better than they? I'm one of hundreds. I'm a woman among millions of women. I know all about it. — But I'm sick, Oscar. I'm sick unto death. I'm sick with love. I'm nearer to death than to life. It's all your doing, and you can save me without sacrificing anything, without assuming any burden. Why can't you then?

GERARDO: *(Emphasizing every word.)* Because my contract binds me not to marry or to travel in the company of women.

HELEN: *(Perplexed.)* But what could possibly prevent you?

GERARDO: My contract.

HELEN: You mean you're not allowed to — ?

GERARDO: I'm not allowed to marry before my contract has expired.

HELEN: And you're not allowed to — ?

GERARDO: — to travel in the company of women.

HELEN: I don't understand such a thing. Whom could it possibly concern?

GERARDO: My manager.

HELEN: Your manager? What business could it be of his?

GERARDO: It *is* his business.

HELEN: You mean because it might — affect your — voice?

GERARDO: Yes.

HELEN: But that's childish. — *Does* it affect your voice?

GERARDO: No.

HELEN: Does your manager believe in this nonsense?

GERARDO: No, he doesn't believe in it either.

HELEN: I don't understand. I can't comprehend how a — respectable human being could sign such a contract!

GERARDO: I am an artist first — and then I am a human being.

HELEN: Yes, I believe you. You're a great artist. An eminent artist. Then why can't you understand that I love you? Is this the only thing that your great mind can't understand? — I'm contemptible to you because you're the only man who has ever made me feel his superiority, the only man I've ever wanted to please. I did everything to hide from you what you meant to me — I was afraid of boring you. But yesterday I experienced what no woman should ever have to endure. If I weren't so in love with you, Oscar, you'd think more of me. That's the most terrible thing about you. You despise the woman whose whole world you are. I'm nothing now, nothing but an empty shell. Now that your passion has consumed me, you want to leave me here like this. But my life will go with you, Oscar. So take along this flesh and blood, too — it belongs to you — unless you want it to perish.

GERARDO: Helen —

HELEN: Your contract! What are contracts to you! Who ever heard of a contract that couldn't be gotten around in some way! Why are contracts made? You mustn't use your contract as a weapon to murder me. I don't believe in your contracts. Let me go with you, Oscar. You'll see, he won't even mention breach of contract. He won't, I know he won't, I know human nature. And if he does, then there will always be time for me to die.

GERARDO: But we have no right to each other, Helen. You're no more free to follow me, than I'm free to take such a responsibility upon myself. — I don't even belong to myself. I belong to my art —

HELEN: Your art, your art! What could I possibly care about your art! I've clung to your art only so you'd pay attention to me. Could heaven make a man like you, to let him make a fool of himself night after night? How can you boast about it? You can see I'm willing to ignore that you're an artist. What couldn't one ignore in a demigod like you. If you were a criminal, Oscar, I'd feel the same about you. I can't control myself. I lie in the dust before you as I should always lie. I should always entreat your mercy as I entreat it now. I should always be lost in you as I am lost at this moment. And death should always be before my eyes as it stands there now.

GERARDO: *(Laughing.)* Helen, Helen! What's all this about death! Women as capable of enjoying life as you are can't commit suicide. You know the value of life better than I. You're too sensible to throw your life away. You should leave that for others to do — half human beasts and dwarfs — the ones nature has treated like stepchildren.

HELEN: Oscar — I never said I was going to shoot myself. When did I ever say such a thing? Where would I get the courage? I said I'd die unless you took me with you; die in the way a person dies of any sickness, because I'm only alive when I'm with you. I can live without everything else — without home, without children — but not without you. I simply can't live without you.

GERARDO: *(Uneasy.)* Helen — calm yourself. Or you'll force me to do something terrible. I have exactly ten more minutes. This scene you're making is not sufficient for me to break my contract. Your state of mind will not justify me in front of any judge. I can give you ten minutes more. If in that time you can't control yourself, Helen — well, I simply can't leave you in this condition.

HELEN: I don't care if the whole world sees me lying here.

GERARDO: Consider the risk you're taking.

HELEN: As if I still had anything to risk.

GERARDO: Your social position.

HELEN: All I can lose is you.

GERARDO: And your family?

HELEN: My family doesn't exist except for you.

GERARDO: But I don't belong to you.

HELEN: I have nothing to lose but my life.

GERARDO: And your children?

HELEN: *(Flaring up.)* Who took me away from them, Oscar? Who robbed my children of their mother?

GERARDO: Did I make advances to you?

HELEN: *(With the greatest passion.)* No, no! You must never believe that! I threw myself at you then and I would throw myself at you now! Neither my husband nor my children could have held me back! If I die, then I'll have known what life is, Oscar! Through you! I have you to thank that I've come to know myself! And I do thank you for it, Oscar! I do!

GERARDO: Helen — listen to me quietly.

HELEN: Yes. Yes. We still have ten minutes.

GERARDO: Listen to me quietly.

(They both sit on the divan.)

HELEN: *(Staring at him.)* I have you to thank for it.

GERARDO: Helen —

HELEN: I'm not asking for you to love me. All I ask is to breathe the same air as you.

GERARDO: *(Struggling to maintain his composure.)* Helen — a man like me can't be bound by the conventional ways of life. I've known society women in every country of Europe. And they've always made scenes when it came time for me to leave. Yet we always knew what we owed to our positions. But I've never been faced with an outburst such as yours. — Helen — not a day goes by but I'm tempted to run off to some idyllic Arcadia with one woman or another. But one must always be conscious of his duty. You're bound by duty the same as I. And there's no higher law than duty.

****

from **The Marquis of Keith** (1901)
from Act Five

CHARACTERS

Keith

Ernst Scholz

[Keith is a con man from a lower-class family masquerading as an aristocrat. Ernst Scholz, a childhood friend, is an aristocrat born into wealth who has chosen to renounce his heritage. Earlier in the play, Keith convinced three Munich businessman to invest in a "Fairyland Palace" — a Disneyland-type entertainment facility. But instead of investing the money, Keith pocketed the cash and spent it on himself. His deception has now been discovered, and in this act, he tries to convince Scholz to lend him the money to rescue his enterprise.]

Munich. Keith's elegant study.

KEITH: *(Alone, wrenched by heart spasms.)* — Ah! — Ah! — I'm dying! — *(Lunges for the writing table, removes a handful of letters from the drawer and hurries toward the door.)* Anna! Anna! *(In the open doorway he is met by Scholz who walks without even a trace of his injury. He starts back.)* I was just going to your hotel.

SCHOLZ: No sense in that. I'm leaving.

KEITH: Then at least give me the twenty thousand marks you promised me yesterday!

SCHOLZ: There'll be no more money from me.

KEITH: The caryatids are crushing me! They want to strip me of my directorship!

SCHOLZ: Then that confirms me in my resolution.

KEITH: It's a momentary crisis, is all! I can handle it!

SCHOLZ: My wealth is more important to me than you! My wealth secures for the members of my family a free and lofty position of power for all time! You, on the other hand, will never be of use to *any*one!

KEITH: Parasite! How *dare* accuse you me of being useless?

SCHOLZ: Let's not argue! — I'm finally making that great renunciation that many a man must agree to in this life.

KEITH: And what's that?

SCHOLZ: I've torn free of all my illusions.

KEITH: *(Scornfully.)* Wallowing in the love of another lower-class girl?

SCHOLZ: I've torn free of everything. — I'm entering a private sanatorium.

KEITH: *(Screaming.)* There is nothing more shameful than being a traitor to your own self!

SCHOLZ: I can well understand your anger. These last three days I've fought the most terrible battle that a mere mortal can endure.

KEITH: To crawl away a coward at the end? — As victor to renounce your worth as a human being?

SCHOLZ: *(Flaring into a rage.)* I am *not* renouncing my worth as a human being! You have no cause to insult me, to jeer at me! — If a man forces himself, *against his will*, to accept the restraints I put upon myself now, *then* he may very *well* lose his worth as a human being. And yet, because of that, he remains relatively happy; he protects his illusions. — A man who comes to terms with reality dispassionately, as I am, resigns neither the respect nor the sympathy of his fellow men.

KEITH: *(Shrugs his shoulders.)* I'd take a little more time to think it over.

SCHOLZ: I've given it mature consideration. It's the last duty my destiny requires me to fulfill.

KEITH: Once you're in, getting out won't be so easy.

SCHOLZ: If I had even the slightest hope of getting out again, I'd never go in. The renunciation that I've burdened myself with, the self-conquest and joyful hope that I've wrested from my soul, I undertook in order to change my fate. I bewail God that there is no longer any doubt that I am different from other men.

KEITH: *(Very proudly.)* And I *praise* God that I have never *doubted* that I was different from other men!

SCHOLZ: *(Very calmly.)* Bewail God or praise God — until this very moment I have thought of you as the most cunning of scoundrels! — But I've given up even this illusion. A scoundrel counts on luck just as surely as an honorable man counts on good conscience not deserting him even in irrevocable misfortune. Your luck is as threadbare as mine, except that you don't know it. That's the horrible danger hanging over you!

KEITH: The only danger hanging over me is that tomorrow I'm out of money!

SCHOLZ: None of your tomorrows will have money, no matter how long you live! — I wish I knew you were safe from the hopeless consequences of your delusion. It's why I've come to see you this last time. I'm profoundly convinced that the best thing for you is to come with me.

KEITH: *(Cunningly.)* Where?

SCHOLZ: To the sanatorium.

KEITH: Give me the thirty thousand marks and I'll be right there with you.

SCHOLZ: Come with me and there will be no more need of money — ever. You'll find a more comfortable life than you may ever have known. We'll keep a carriage and horses, we'll play billiards —

KEITH: *(Embracing him.)* Give me the thirty thousand marks!! Shall I humiliate myself here at your feet? I could be arrested on the spot!

SCHOLZ: So it's gone that far, has it? *(Pushing him back.)* I don't give sums like that to madmen!

KEITH: *(Shouts.)* You're the madman!

SCHOLZ: *(Calmly.)* I'm the one come to his senses.

KEITH: *(Scornfully.)* If a lunatic asylum lures you because you've come to your senses — go right ahead!

SCHOLZ: You're one they have to bring there by force!

KEITH: — I suppose you'll reassume your title once you're there?

SCHOLZ: You've gone bankrupt on two continents in every conceivable way that bourgeois life permits!

KEITH: *(Venomously.)* If it is your moral duty to free the world of your superfluous existence, I'm sure there are more radical means than going for drives and playing billiards!

SCHOLZ: I tried that long ago.

KEITH: *(Shouts at him.)* Then what are you still doing here?!

SCHOLZ: *(Gloomily.)* I failed at that as I have at everything else.

KEITH: May I suppose you shot someone else — by mistake?

SCHOLZ: They cut the bullets from between my shoulders; near the spinal column. — This is the last time anyone will ever offer you a helping hand. You already know the sort of experiences that are in store for you.

KEITH: *(Throws himself on his knees and clasps Scholz's hands.)* — Give me the forty thousand marks and I'm saved!

SCHOLZ: That won't save you from the penitentiary!

KEITH: *(Starts up in terror.)* Shut up!

SCHOLZ: *(Pleading.)* Come with me and you'll be safe. We grew up together; why shouldn't we wait for the end together, too? To bourgeois society you're a criminal and subject to all kinds of inhuman medieval tortures —

KEITH: *(Moaning.)* If you won't help me, then go, please, I beg of you!

SCHOLZ: *(Tears in his eyes.)* You mustn't turn your back on your only refuge! You didn't choose your pitiable fate anymore than I chose mine.

KEITH: Go! Go!

SCHOLZ: Come. Come. — As a companion I'll be gentle as a lamb. It would be a dim ray in the dark night of my life to rescue my boyhood friend from his terrible fate.

KEITH: Go! Please!

SCHOLZ: — I want you to entrust yourself to my guidance as of this moment — as I once wanted to entrust myself to you —

KEITH: *(Cries out in despair.)* Sasha! Sasha!

SCHOLZ: At least, then, don't forget that — that you have a friend who will welcome you at any time. *(Goes off.)*

****

from **Pandora's Box** (1904)
from Act Two

CHARACTERS

Schigolch

Lulu

[Lulu was convicted of the murder of her husband, Schön, and has escaped prison. Rodrigo Quast, an acrobat, wants to maker her into a trapeze artist, while Count Casti-Piani is threatening to turn her into the police unless she becomes a prostitute in Cairo. Schigolch, a father figure and sometime protector for Lulu, has come to visit her. Here, she pleads with him to help her out of her predicament.]

Paris. A spacious salon. Schigolch enters through the gaming room, heads straight for an armchair, and lowers himself exhaustedly into it.

SCHIGOLCH: *(To Lulu.)* I need five hundred francs. To furnish an apartment, For my — mistress. *Elle veut se mettre dans ses meubles.*

LULU: Good God! A mistress? You?

SCHIGOLCH: With God's good help.

LULU: But you're — eighty!

SCHIGOLCH: What else is Paris good for?

LULU: My God!

SCHIGOLCH: She's no spring chicken, either.

LULU: Merciful heaven!

SCHIGOLCH: I've wasted too much of my life in Germany.

LULU: I — dear God —

SCHIGOLCH: You haven't laid eyes on me for six weeks.

LULU: I — I — I can't anymore — I can't anymore — it's too — too —

SCHIGOLCH: Too what?

LULU: Too — horrible! *(Breaks down, buries her head on his knees and shakes with convulsive sobs.)* It's — too — horrible!

SCHIGOLCH: I was in the clink the whole time. *(Stroking her hair.)* You drive yourself too hard. You need to let up for a few days.

LULU: Oh! — Oh! — How have I — deserved this! What have I — done! Oh — God in heaven! Oh, God, oh, God — what will — become of me! — Oh, the things I've suffered! — Merciful God! I can't take this anymore! — I can't go through it! Oh — it's too — horrible!

SCHIGOLCH: They freed me only yesterday. *(Stroking her.)* You should wash yourself in snow. Cry it out if it helps you any. Go on.

LULU: *(Groaning.)* Oh! — Oh! — Oh, God — oh, God!

SCHIGOLCH: I learned a little French in the clink. You should take salt baths. Cry it out. Go on. Spend one day a week in bed with a novel.

LULU: What will become of me! Oh! What will become of me!

SCHIGOLCH: It'll be over soon. Just cry it out. I haven't had you on my knee like this for — good lord! — twenty years. How time flies! How you've grown! You cried the same way then. I had you here. I stroked your hair and rubbed your knees warm. Of course you had no white satin dress then, no feathers in your hair, no see-through stockings. You had no stockings at all. Scarcely a shirt to your name. But crying — that was something you knew how to do.

LULU: Please! Please take me with you! Take me! Please! Have pity on me! Take me with you! Now! Take me — back to your attic!

SCHIGOLCH: Me? Take you with me?

LULU: To your attic! To your attic!

SCHIGOLCH: And my — my five hundred francs?

LULU: Oh, God!

SCHIGOLCH: You live too much for pleasure. More than you can endure. You need to allow your body time to — to find peace again.

LULU: They want my life.

SCHIGOLCH: Who wants your life? Who? Who?

LULU: They're going to betray me.

SCHIGOLCH: Who's going to betray you? Tell me.

LULU: They're going to — oh!

SCHIGOLCH: What?

LULU: Cut off my head! Cut off my head!

SCHIGOLCH: Who's going to cut off your head? I may be eighty years
old, but —

LULU: I can see myself tied in their ropes!

SCHIGOLCH: Who wants to cut off your head?

LULU: Rodrigo! Rodrigo Quast!

SCHIGOLCH: Him?

LULU: He told me so just now.

SCHIGOLCH: Don't lose sleep over that. I'll take him out to a bar.

LULU: Kill him! Oh, please! Kill him! Kill him! You can do it — if you
want to!

SCHIGOLCH: He's a gigolo. He says all kinds of things he doesn't
mean.

LULU: Kill him! Kill him!

SCHIGOLCH: He tries to look important.

LULU: For your child's sake! Kill him!

SCHIGOLCH: I don't know — whose child you are.

LULU: I won't get up till you've given me your word.

SCHIGOLCH: The poor devil.

LULU: Kill him!

SCHIGOLCH: Once he's gone — you can't bring him back. I could
throw him out my window into the Seine.

LULU: Please!

SCHIGOLCH: And what do I get out of it?

LULU: Do it! Do it!

SCHIGOLCH: What do I get out of it?

LULU: Five hundred francs.

SCHIGOLCH: Five hundred francs. Five hundred francs.

LULU: A thousand.

SCHIGOLCH: If I really wanted to put my hand to this — here in
Paris — I could be rich again.

LULU: How much do you want?

SCHIGOLCH: I could drive around in style again, no matter what my age.

LULU: How much? How much?

SCHIGOLCH: If you could manage to —

LULU: Me?

SCHIGOLCH: — lower yourself to —

LULU: God have pity on me!

SCHIGOLCH: — like you used to —

LULU: With — you?

SCHIGOLCH: Now, of course, you have beautiful clothes.

LULU: What do you want — with me!

SCHIGOLCH: You'll see.

LULU: I'm not — like — I was then.

SCHIGOLCH: You think I'm an antique?

LULU: But you've got someone.

SCHIGOLCH: The little lady's sixty-five years old.

LULU: What do you do, then?

SCHIGOLCH: Play patience.

LULU: And — with me?

SCHIGOLCH: You'll see.

LULU: You're a brute.

SCHIGOLCH: It's been so long since we've known each other.

LULU: For — God's — sake.

SCHIGOLCH: We'll renew old memories.

LULU: *(Getting up.)* But you swear to me that —

SCHIGOLCH: When will you come?

LULU: Merciful heaven!

SCHIGOLCH: Just so I'm alone.

LULU: Whenever you want.

SCHIGOLCH: Day after tomorrow.

LULU: If I have to.

SCHIGOLCH: In white satin.

LULU: But you *will* throw him in?

SCHIGOLCH: With diamonds and pearls.

LULU: Just as I am now.

SCHIGOLCH: Just once more — to make the earth shake.

LULU: You swear.

SCHIGOLCH: Just send him.

LULU: You swear, you swear.

SCHIGOLCH: By all things holy.

LULU: You'll throw him in.

SCHIGOLCH: I swear.

LULU: By all things holy.

SCHIGOLCH: *(Feeling around under her dress.)* What more do you want?

LULU: *(Trembling.)* By all things — holy.

SCHIGOLCH: By all things holy.

LULU: How that cools me!

SCHIGOLCH: *(Letting go of the dress.)* You're blazing with hate.

(Pause. Lulu goes stage left, puts her dress in order, straightens her hair at the mirror, and dries her eyes.)

LULU: Go now — right now — go.

SCHIGOLCH: Today?

LULU: Just be sure you're home when he comes with her.

SCHIGOLCH: With who?

LULU: *(Feeling her cheeks and powdering them.)* He's coming with the Countess.

SCHIGOLCH: A Countess?

LULU: Get them to drink. Tell him it's the Countess's room — that you live next door. The Countess will get drunk. Put something into his drink. Whatever you've got.

SCHIGOLCH: It'll turn the trick.

LULU: I only hope you can lift him. God — oh, God.

SCHIGOLCH: Three steps to the window.

LULU: In the morning the Countess will silently steal away.

SCHIGOLCH: What if I have to roll him?

LULU: She'll never recognize the house again.

SCHIGOLCH: My window goes clear to the floor.

LULU: Don't forget. Bring me his earrings.

SCHIGOLCH: Once he's overboard, I'll bid a fond farewell to the old hole in the wall.

LULU: You hear? His golden ear — rings.

SCHIGOLCH: What is it?

LULU: I think —

SCHIGOLCH: What in the name of —

LULU: I think — my garter —

SCHIGOLCH: Why are you staring at me?

LULU: My garter — broke.

SCHIGOLCH: So then I'll look for a place behind the Bastille. *(Lulu has pulled up her dress and is tying her garter.)* Or else behind the Buttes-Chaumont. Yellow stockings.

LULU: Orange.

SCHIGOLCH: What a lovely smell!

LULU: Everything orange — to white satin. *(Straightening up.)* Go — go on now.

SCHIGOLCH: Orange. Hm! Who's this Countess of yours?

LULU: The crazy woman. You know her. You need to take a cab.

SCHIGOLCH: Of course I do. Of course! *(Getting up.)* What crazy woman?

LULU: The one who kisses my feet. Please, go.

SCHIGOLCH: *(As he goes off.)* His golden earrings.

(Lulu leads him off upstage left.)

****

Wedekind

THE READING ROOM

YOUNG ACTORS AND THEIR TEACHERS
Brooks, Louise. *Lulu in Hollywood*. New York: Knopf, 1982.

SCHOLARS, STUDENTS, PROFESSORS

Blei, Franz. *Über Wedekind: Sternheim und das Theater*. Leipzig: K. Wolff, 1915.

Elster, Hanns Martin. *Wedekind und seine besten Bühnenwerke*. Berlin and Leipzig: Franz Schneider, 1922.

Fechter, Paul. *Frank Wedekind. Der Mensch und das Werk*. Jena: Erich Lichtenstein, 1920.

Friedmann, Jürgen. *Frank Wedekinds Dramen nach 1900*. Stuttgart: Hans-Dieter Heinz, 1975.

Gay, Peter, ed. *The Freud Reader*. New York and London: Norton, 1989.

Höger, Alfons. *Frank Wedekind. Der Konstruktivismus als schöpferische Methode*. Königstein: Scriptor, 1979.

Irmer, Hans-Jochen. *Der Theaterdichter Frank Wedekind: Werk und Wirkung*. Berlin: Henschelverlag, 1975.

Kapp, Julius. *Frank Wedekind. Seine Eigenart und seine Werke*. Berlin: Hermann Barsdorf, 1909.

Keiser, Rolf. *Benjamin Franklin Wedekind. Biographie einer Jugend*. Zurich: Arche, 1990.

Kempner, Hans. *Frank Wedekind als Mensch und Künstler*. Berlin-Pankow: Oskar Linser, 1911.

Kim, Kwangsun. *Die Lieder in Frank Wedekinds Dramen*. Frankfurt-am-Main and Berlin: Lang, 1993.

Kuhn, Anna Katharina. *Der Dialog bei Frank Wedekind*. Heidelberg: Karl Winter, 1981.

This extensive bibliography lists books about the playwright according to whom the books might be of interest. If you would like to research further something that interests you in the text, lists of references, sources cited, and editions used in this book are found in this section.

Kutscher, Artur. *Frank Wedekind. Sein Leben und seine Werke.* 3 vols. New York: AMS Press, 1970. [Reprint of the original publication of 1922, 1927, and 1931.]

Medicus, Thoman. *Die grosse Liebe. Ökonomie und Konstruktion der Körper im Werk von Frank Wedekind.* Marburg an der Lahn: Guttandin & Hoppe, 1982.

Pissin, Raimund. *Frank Wedekind.* Berlin: Gose & Tetzlaff, 1905.

Seehaus, Günther. *Frank Wedekind und das Theater.* Munich: Laocoon, 1964.

Ude, Karl. *Frank Wedekind.* Mühlacker: Stieglitz Verlag, 1966.

Vinçon, Hartmut. *Frank Wedekind.* Stuttgart: Metzler, 1987.

Völker, Klaus. *Frank Wedekind.* Velber bei Hanover: Friedrich Verlag, 1965.

ACTORS, DIRECTORS, PROFESSIONALS

Diethe, Carol. *Aspects of Distorted Sexual Attitudes in German Expressionist Drama.* New York, Bern, Frankfurt-am-Main, and Paris: Lang, 1988.

Esslin, Martin. *The Theatre of the Absurd.* London and New York: Penguin Books, 1991.

Mueller, Rüdiger H. *Sex, Love and Prostitution in Turn-of-the-Century German-Language Drama,* Frankfurt-am-Main: Peter Lang, 2006.

Pascal, Roy. *From Naturalism to Expressionism, German Literature and Society 1880–1918.* London: Weidenfels & Nicolson, 1974.

Peacock, Ronald. "The Ambiguity of Wedekind's Lulu." *Oxford German Studies,* 9, 1978.

Shaw, Leroy R. *The Playwright and Historical Change.* Madison: University of Wisconsin Press, 1970.

Skrine, Peter, *Hauptmann, Wedekind, and Schnitzler.* New York: St. Martin's Press, 1989.

Spalter, Max. *Brecht's Tradition.* Baltimore: Johns Hopkins, 1967.

Willett, John. *Expressionism.* London: Weidenfels & Nicolson, 1970.

THE EDITIONS OF WEDEKIND'S WORKS USED FOR THIS BOOK

Wedekind, Frank, *Four Major Plays.* Vol. I. Translated by Carl R. Mueller. Lyme, NH: Smith and Kraus, 2000.

Wedekind, Frank, *Four Plays.* Vol. II. Translated by Carl R. Mueller. Lyme, NH: Smith and Kraus, 2002.

SOURCES CITED IN THIS BOOK

Best, Alan. *Frank Wedekind.* London: Oswald Wolff, 1975.

Boa, Elizabeth. *The Sexual Circus: Wedekind's Theatre of Subversion.* London: Basil Blackwell, 1987.

Garten, H. F. *Modern German Drama.* 2nd ed. London: Methuen, 1964.

Gittleman, Sol. *Frank Wedekind.* New York: Twayne, 1969.

Kayser, Wolfgang. *The Grotesque in Art and Literature.* New York: Columbia University Press, 1981.

Keynes, John Maynard. *Essays in Persuasion.* New York: Norton, 1963.

Lewis, Ward B. *The Ironic Dissident: Frank Wedekind in the View of His Critics.* Columbia: Camden House, 1997.

Marcuse, Herbert. *Eros and Civilization.* Boston: Beacon Press, 1974.

INDEX

The entries in the index include highlights from the main In an Hour essay portion of the book.

ABOUT THE AUTHOR

Carl Mueller was a professor in the Department of Theater at the University of California, Los Angeles, from 1967 until his death in 2008. There he directed and taught theater history, criticism, dramatic literature, and playwriting. He was educated at Northwestern University, where he received a B.S. in English. After work in graduate English at the University of California, Berkeley, he received his M.A. in Playwriting at UCLA, where he also completed his Ph.D. in Theater History and Criticism, In 1960–1961 he was a Fulbright Scholar in Berlin.

A translator for more than forty years, he translated and published works by Büchner, Brecht, Wedekind, Hauptmann, Hofmannsthal, and Hebbel, to name a few. His published translation of von Horváth's *Tales from the Vienna Woods* was given its London West End premiere in July 1999. For Smith and Kraus he translated individual volumes of plays by Schnitzler, Strindberg, Pirandello, Kleist, and Wedekind. His translation of Goethe's *Faust Part One* and *Part Two* appeared in 2004. He also translated for Smith and Kraus *Sophokles: The Complete Plays* (2000), a two-volume *Aeschylus: The Complete Plays* (2002), and a four volume *Euripides: The Complete Plays* (2005). His translations have been performed in every English-speaking country and have appeared on BBC-TV.

Smith and Kraus wishes to thank Hugh Denard, whose enlightened permissions policy reflects an understanding that copyright law is intended to both protect the rights of creators of intellectual property as well as to encourage its use for the public good.

Know the playwright, love the play.

Open a new door to theater study, performance, and audience satisfaction with these Playwrights In an Hour titles.

ANCIENT GREEK

Aeschylus   Aristophanes   Euripides   Sophocles

RENAISSANCE

William Shakespeare

MODERN

Anton Chekhov   Noël Coward   Lorraine Hansberry
Henrik Ibsen   Arthur Miller   Molière   Eugene O'Neill
Arthur Schnitzler   George Bernard Shaw   August Strindberg
Frank Wedekind   Oscar Wilde   Thornton Wilder
Tennessee Williams

CONTEMPORARY

Edward Albee   Alan Ayckbourn   Samuel Beckett
Theresa Rebeck   Sarah Ruhl   Sam Shepard   Tom Stoppard
August Wilson

To purchase or for more information
visit our web site inanhourbooks.com